SOLUTIONS

TO SELECTED EXERCISES IN

COMPUTER ARCHITECTURE
A
QUANTITATIVE
APPROACH

THOMAS E. WILLIS

ALLAN D. KNIES

MORGAN KAUFMANN PUBLISHERS, INC., SAN FRANCISCO, CALIFORNIA

Sponsoring Editors	Bruce M. Spatz, Jennifer Mann
Production Manager	Yonie Overton
Production Editor	Julie Pabst
Editorial Assistant	Jane Elliott
Cover Design	Carron Design
Proofreader	Erin Milnes
Printer	Edwards Brothers, Inc.

This book was typeset by the authors in LaTeX.

Morgan Kaufmann Publishers, Inc.
Editorial and Sales Office
340 Pine Street, Sixth Floor
San Francisco, CA 94104-3205
USA

Telephone	(415) 392-2665
Facsimile	(415) 982-2665
Internet	`mkp@mkp.com`
Order toll free	(800) 745-7323

Library of Congress Cataloging-in-Publication Data is available for this book.

ISBN 1-55860-406-5

A Note from the Publisher

Accompanying the second edition of *Computer Architecture: A Quantitative Approach* is a wealth of supplementary materials. In addition to the solutions to selected exercises provided in this manual, a comprehensive guide to the DLX architecture is available. The *DLX Instruction Set Architecture Handbook*, by Philip M. Sailer and David R. Kaeli, provides complete information on the details of DLX. It is an indispensable reference for readers of *Computer Architecture: A Quantitative Approach*. If you would like to purchase a copy of this handbook, please contact us by email at `orders@mkp.com` or by phone at (800) 745-7323.

Additional support materials for *Computer Architecture: A Quantitative Approach, Second Edition*, are available at our Web site at `http://mkp.com`. Here you will find the DLX and related software, figures from the text, errata, lecture slides, and course notes developed by instructors using the text. We will be adding new materials to this site over time, so please be sure to check it periodically.

Contents

Introduction

This solution manual for the second edition of *Computer Architecture: A Quantitative Approach* is intended to provide you with example solutions for many of the problems in the text. The manual covers all eight chapters of CA:AQA in addition to the two appendices that include exercises. In most instances, solutions are provided with enough explanation in addition to the answer that you should be able to understand the process by which the exercise was solved.

How Were the Exercises Selected?

Due to the fact that some exercises in the text, such as programming assignments, have a multitude of answers, we have only solved a subset of the exercises. Exercises were selected based on the idea that our solutions should reflect the way you should go about solving for a specific answer. Thus, questions for which the range of answers is very large, or for which in-depth discussion is required, were generally omitted. These types of problems include most programming exercises, discussion questions, and some analysis/proof questions. We also selected exercises we felt were representative of the types of problems you might encounter in the text and for which the solutions provide a good explanation of general problem-solving techniques.

How Is This Manual Organized Anyway?

The ten chapters in this manual correspond to the eight chapters and first two appendices of the second edition of *Computer Architecture: A Quantitative Approach*. As mentioned above, each chapter begins with a brief overview before presenting the exercise solutions. Within each chapter, known inconsistencies in the problems have been pointed out either at the beginning of the chapter or at the beginning of the solution for affected exercises.

Some General Problem-Solving Strategies

Given the broad scope of the text, it is difficult to present solution strategies that apply to all of the exercises in CA:AQA. However, in solving hundreds of the exercises, we have developed a good feel for general strategies that can be helpful. Along with the general strategies that follow, the solutions attempt to also illustrate how specific types of exercises can be solved.

Remember, It Is a Quantitative Approach

It is helpful to remember the title of the text when thinking about how to approach an exercise. As the text advocates a quantitative approach to computer architecture, you should try to focus on using such measures in your solutions. Most of the quantitative measurements developed in Chapter 1, such as CPI and CPU time, are heavily used *throughout* the text. We encourage you to make sure that you have a clear understanding of the concepts in Chapter 1 before moving on to later chapters.

Relevant Section Numbers

The section numbers delimited by angle brackets in the exercise statements in the text can be helpful in identifying which assumptions are appropriate to make. For example, in Chapters 3 and 4 on pipelining, the authors present several architectural variations. The section numbers can clarify exactly which of the variations discussed in the text to use.

Making Assumptions

In some exercises, there are several reasonable assumptions that can be made within the framework of the exercise. As mentioned earlier, we have attempted to identify such exercises and assumptions. In such cases where there does not seem to be one correct interpretation, we encourage you to make a reasonable assumption and avoid becoming hung up wondering exactly what the authors are after.

Pipeline Diagrams

When solving some of the exercises that relate to pipeline performance, it is often helpful to draw pipeline diagrams such as Figure 3.8 in the text. We have found these figures to be of great value in evaluating exactly what occurs in the pipeline in various situations.

Closing Remarks & Acknowledgements

Writing this manual has proven to be an interesting experience for both of us. What we initially thought would be a week's worth of intense work doing a gamma review of CA:AQA turned into an offer to write this manual and provide feedback on the exercises themselves. Although the offer came at a time that found us both very busy in various stages of dissertation writing, we agreed to take on the project.

Several individuals took the time to inform of us of bugs they had noticed while using one of the beta editions of this manual that were released over the past few months. We appreciate their time and effort to help make this manual accurate: George Adams, Jay DeSouza, Alex Garthwaite, Gyula Mago, Dinesh Mehta, Oskar Mencer, Dyke Stiles, and Ralph Tindell. The solutions in this manual have also been used at Purdue in EE565, a graduate-level computer architecture class. We would like to thank the students of EE565 for providing comments and feedback on the solutions. Finally, Jane Elliott, Jennifer Mann, Julie Pabst, and Bruce Spatz at Morgan Kaufmann all helped out with various facets of the publishing end of this manual. We greatly appreciate their understanding and efforts to make the entire process go as smoothly as possible.

We hope that you find the manual useful.

Allan Knies (`aknies@mipos2.intel.com`)
Tom Willis (`twillis@ecn.purdue.edu`)

Chapter 1

Fundamentals of Computer Design

Introduction to the Chapter 1 Exercises

Chapter 1 develops the quantitative foundation that later chapters build upon. The chapter begins by examining some of the technology and cost issues that drive computer architecture and concludes by discussing how you could go about reporting and measuring computer system performance. Within the chapter, Sections 1.5–1.7 develop the basic analysis equations and techniques that are applied throughout the text. A clear understanding of the concepts presented in these sections is critical given their usage throughout the text.

▷ Exercise 1.1

Each part of this exercise uses Amdahl's Law to explore aspects of the performance benefits of a vector mode that improves system performance for some types of computations (see Appendix B of the text for more information on vectors). From Section 1.6 of the text, Amdahl's Law is given by

$$Speedup_{overall} = \frac{1}{(1 - Fraction_{enhanced}) + \left(\frac{Fraction_{enhanced}}{Speedup_{enhanced}} \right)} \qquad (1.1)$$

The key thing to remember about Amdahl's Law is that it shows that the speedup you can achieve through an enhancement is limited by the amount of time the code operates in the unenhanced mode.

5

▷ Exercise 1.1(a)

This exercise illustrates how hard it is for an optimization to pay off under the constraints of Amdahl's Law as presented in Equation 1.1. Specifically, in this exercise we investigate the potential benefits gained through adding a vector mode to a hypothetical machine by plotting the relationship between utilization of the vector mode and speedup. The first step in the solution is to reduce Equation 1.1 by plugging in 20 for the value of the speedup possible from vector mode, $Speedup_{enhanced}$. Doing a bit of algebra yields the following equation:

$$Speedup_{overall} = \frac{20}{20 - 19\,(Fraction_{enhanced})}$$

The exercise asks us to plot the behavior of the speedup, $Speedup_{overall}$, as the percentage of vectorization, $Fraction_{enhanced}$, increases. Note that $Fraction_{enhanced}$ refers to the amount of time in the *unoptimized* system that can take advantage of a vector mode.

Plotting $Speedup_{overall}$ versus $Fraction_{enhanced}$ yields the plot shown in Figure 1.1. The "exponential" shape of this curve shows that the optimization does not begin to pay off until large percentages of code can be run in vector mode. Even at levels of vectorization of 75%, the overall speedup is almost an *order of magnitude* less than the maximum speedup possible with the vector unit. Essentially, until the time that you spend in the unoptimized mode accounts for a small percentage of the total time, it severely limits the speedup. This plot shows the futility of adding a fast mode that can not be used frequently and leads to a very common rule of thumb in computer architecture: "Make the common case fast."

▷ Exercise 1.1(c)

From the exercise statement, we know that the maximum speedup possible from the vector optimization is 20. The exercise asks for the level of vectorization required to achieve one-half of the maximum speedup. The answer can be found by solving Amdahl's Law, shown in Equation 1.1, for $Fraction_{enhanced}$. Plugging the values given in the exercise statement, 10 for $Speedup_{overall}$ (one-half of the maximum speedup) and 20 for $Speedup_{enhanced}$, into Equation 1.1 yields the result:

$$10 = \frac{1}{(1 - Fraction_{enhanced}) + \left(\frac{Fraction_{enhanced}}{20}\right)}$$

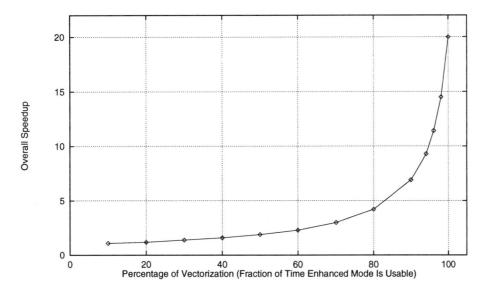

Figure 1.1: Overall Speedup versus Percentage of Vectorization.

$$Fraction_{enhanced} \quad = \quad \frac{18}{19} = 0.95$$

Thus, to get one-half of the potential speedup, the system must be able to use vector mode 95% of the time! This result should help you appreciate just how hard Amdahl's Law makes life for computer architects.

▷ Exercise 1.2

This question further explores the effects of Amdahl's Law, but the data given in the question are given in a form that can not be directly applied to the general speedup formula.

▷ Exercise 1.2(a)

In this exercise, we are trying to find the speedup of the new system, which has an enhanced mode that is 10 times faster than normal mode. However, in this exercise, we are not given information in the correct form to directly apply Amdahl's law. Thus, we start by stating the basic definition of speedup:

$$Speedup = \frac{Time_{unenhanced}}{Time_{enhanced}}$$

We are told that 50% of the execution time of our program on the improved system is spent running the portion of the code that has been enhanced by the change. Translating the previous sentence directly into an equation gives

$$\frac{1}{2} Time_{enhanced} = \frac{Percent_{original} \times Time_{unenhanced}}{10} \tag{1.2}$$

$Percent_{original}$ is the percentage of the original system that the portion of the code that has been enhanced took originally. The left-hand side of Equation 1.2 reflects "50% of the execution time," while the right-hand side reflects the amount of time spent executing the code that will be run in enhanced mode in terms of the original percentage of the program divided by the speedup in enhanced mode.

$Time_{enhanced}$ can also be computed as the inverse of the speedup times the original unenhanced time.

$$Time_{enhanced} = \left[\frac{Percent_{original}}{10} + (1 - Percent_{original}) \right] \times Time_{unenhanced}$$

Subtracting Equation 1.2 from this equation for $Time_{enhanced}$, we get

$$\frac{1}{2} Time_{enhanced} = (1 - Percent_{original}) \times Time_{unenhanced} \tag{1.3}$$

Solving Equation 1.2 for $Percent_{original}$:

$$Percent_{original} = \frac{10 \times Time_{enhanced}}{2 \times Time_{unenhanced}}$$

Then substituting the result into Equation 1.3 and solving for $\frac{Time_{unenhanced}}{Time_{enhanced}}$, the answer is

$$Speedup = \frac{Time_{unenhanced}}{Time_{enhanced}} = 5.5$$

▷ Exercise 1.4

In this question, we are asked to evaluate the possibility of adding a new instruction that collapses a memory-load instruction with a dependent ALU instruction into a single instruction. To answer this question, we assume that the only load/ALU instruction pairs replaced in the code stream are those that use their loaded values only once (i.e., all other ALU instructions get their operands from other registers or from normal loads). We are asked to evaluate the new design assuming that the change causes the number of cycles for a branch to increase to 2 and that the register memory ALU operations take 2 clocks to execute.

To evaluate the two versions of DLX, we will compute and compare the CPU time for both approaches. We begin by computing the CPI term of the CPU time equation using an expression derived from those in Section 1.6 of the text:

$$CPI = \sum_{i \in Classes} CPI_i \times \frac{IC_i}{Instruction\ Count}$$
$$= \sum_{i \in Classes} CPI_i \times Frequency_i \qquad (1.4)$$

where the number of cycles required by a class of instruction, CPI_i, and the frequency of each class of instruction, $Frequency_i$, is given in Figure 1.17 of the text.

For the CPI of the original design, we multiply the number of clocks each instruction class requires by the percentage of instructions in the instruction mix of that class:

$$CPI_{original} = (1 \times 43\%) + (2 \times 21\%) + (2 \times 12\%) + (2 \times 24\%) = 1.57$$

On average, an instruction requires 1.57 clocks to execute on the original version of DLX. Thus, the CPU time is given by

$$Time_{orig} = 1.57 \times IC_{orig} \times Clk$$

where IC_{orig} is the instruction count and *Clk* is the clock cycle time on both versions of DLX (recall that the exercise states the clock cycle time is unchanged by the modification).

In the new machine, 25% of the ALU instructions have a paired load instruction that can be removed by taking advantage of the new register-memory ALU instruction format. Removing some loads implies that the frequencies of the operations change from the values given in Figure 1.17. To compute new values, we must first determine how many instructions are executed on the new version of DLX. As the ALU instructions constitute 43% of the instruction mix and 25% of these ALU instructions have a paired load that can be eliminated, the new version of DLX executes $25\% \times 43\% = 11\%$ fewer instructions than the original version of DLX.

We can now compute the CPI of each type of operation on the new machine to find the overall CPI of the "improved" version of DLX. In doing so, we normalize the frequencies of instructions to the instruction count on the new machine. For example, if branches are 24% of the mix on the old version of DLX, they constitute $\frac{24\%}{89\%}$ on the new version of DLX, as the new version executes 89% of the instructions executed by the original machine.

In the new machine, 25% of the ALU instructions use the new ALU register-memory format and thus cost two cycles; the other 75% of the ALU operations still cost only 1 cycle. Thus, the contribution to the new system's CPI due to ALU operations is

$$CPI_{alu} = [(2 \times 25\%) + (1 \times 75\%)] \times \frac{43\%}{89\%} = 0.60$$

The contribution from loads is found by subtracting the percentage of instructions in the new stream that are combined instructions from the original percentage of loads. Since each original load costs 2 clocks, if we multiply by 2, we get the contribution to CPI of the remaining loads in the new instruction stream:

$$CPI_{loads} = 2 \times \left[\frac{21\% - (25\% \times 43\%)}{89\%} \right] = 0.23$$

The contribution to CPI of stores is unchanged:

$$CPI_{stores} = 2 \times \frac{12\%}{89\%} = 0.27$$

The CPI of branches is now more expensive since the cost per branch is 3 cycles instead of 2:

$$CPI_{branches} = 3 \times \frac{24\%}{89\%} = 0.81$$

Again, in each case we have adjusted the operation frequencies to account for the change in the instruction count.

Totaling these CPI components yields the CPI for a version of DLX with register-memory ALU instructions of

$$CPI_{modified} = 0.60 + 0.23 + 0.27 + 0.81 = 1.91$$

Therefore, the CPU time on this version of DLX is

$$\begin{aligned} Time_{new} &= IC_{new} \times 1.91 \times Clk = (89\% \times IC_{orig}) \times 1.91 \times Clk \\ &= 1.70 \times IC_{orig} \times Clk \end{aligned}$$

Instruction Class	Frequency	Cycles	Instruction Accesses	Data Accesses
ALU	43%	1	1	0
Load	21%	2	1	1
Store	12%	2	1	1
Branch	24%	2	1	0

Figure 1.2: An Overview of the Instruction Set Architecture.

Because $Time_{new}$ is larger than $Time_{orig}$, adding register-memory ALU instructions to DLX would not be profitable from a performance standpoint for this instruction mix.

▷ Exercise 1.5

> *It is helpful if you are familiar with the terms "miss rate" and "miss penalty" before attempting this exercise.*

This exercise uses information on instruction behavior in a system with a perfect cache in combination with cache performance data to compute an effective CPI that accounts for the non-idealities in the memory system. Such an approach is a common way to analyze performance. To solve this exercise, we must determine the CPI of a system with and without perfect caches and then compute the speedup between these two CPIs.

Before we can compute the CPI, we need to determine the classes of instructions that can be executed by our machine and their execution frequencies. Such information on the machine's instruction set architecture is presented in Figure 1.17 in the text and summarized here in Figure 1.2. This summary shows for each class of instruction the frequency, number of clock cycles required to execute, and number of instruction and data accesses. As the machine in question is based on a load/store instruction set, only load and store instructions are allowed to perform data accesses.

The CPI over a set of instruction classes is given by

$$
\begin{aligned}
CPI &= \sum_{i \in Classes} CPI_i \times \frac{IC_i}{Instruction\ Count} \\
&= \sum_{i \in Classes} CPI_i \times Frequency_i
\end{aligned}
\tag{1.5}
$$

where $Frequency_i$ is the percentage of instructions executed that fall into instruction class i and CPI_i is the effective CPI for instruction class i from

$$
\begin{aligned}
CPI_i &= CPI_{ideal} + CPI_{stalls} \\
&= CPI_{ideal} + \sum_{s \in Stalls} Frequency_s \times Penalty_s \qquad (1.6)
\end{aligned}
$$

This form of the CPI is similar to the clock cycle term in the CPU performance equation that models memory hierarchy presented in Section 1.7 of the text in that the effective CPI is given by the sum of an "ideal" CPI, CPI_{ideal}, and a term that accounts for the penalty arising from stalls (here, $Frequency_s$ and $Penalty_s$ are the frequency and number of additional cycles spent when stall case s occurs).

Before going on, it is instructive to make a brief comment about the terms in Equation 1.6, specifically CPI_{ideal}. Generally, the "ideal" CPI can be anything. The only requirement is that it not include any of the effects accounted for in the stall term. Typically, this CPI provides the CPI of the system in the absence of some "feature" (e.g., a real memory system), while the stall term accounts for the presence of this same "feature." Equations 1.5 and 1.6 find heavy use throughout the text.

For this exercise the expression for the CPI due to stalls, CPI_{stalls}, accounts for the two potential sources of stalls: cache misses caused by instruction references and cache misses caused by data references.

$$
\begin{aligned}
CPI_{stalls} &= (Accesses_i \times Frequency_{i\_miss} \times Penalty_{i\_miss}) + \\
&\quad (Accesses_d \times Frequency_{d\_miss} \times Penalty_{d\_miss}) \qquad (1.7)
\end{aligned}
$$

where the individual terms represent the number of accesses, frequency of misses, and penalty of a miss for instructions and data references. For a perfect cache the memory system does not stall the CPU, and thus CPI_{stalls} is zero.

Using Equation 1.7 along with the information in Figure 1.2 and the exercise statement we can arrive at the terms for the effective CPI with and without a perfect cache. Summarizing these results yields Figure 1.3. Because the perfect caches have no penalties associated with them, the effective CPI of an instruction class in a system with perfect caches is simply CPI_{ideal}. Using the values in Figure 1.3 in conjunction with Equation 1.5 leads to the CPI for the system with a perfect cache:

$$
\begin{aligned}
CPI_{perfect} &= (1 \times 43\%) + (2 \times 21\%) + (2 \times 12\%) + (2 \times 24\%) \\
&= 1.6 \qquad (1.8)
\end{aligned}
$$

Class	Freq.	CPI$_{ideal}$	Perfect Cache		Real Cache	
			CPI$_{stalls}$	CPI$_i$	CPI$_{stalls}$	CPI$_i$
ALU	43%	1	0	1	2	3
Load	21%	2	0	2	6	8
Store	12%	2	0	2	6	8
Branch	24%	2	0	2	2	4

Figure 1.3: Terms of the Effective CPI Expression.

and the CPI for the system with a real cache:

$$\begin{aligned} CPI_{real} &= (3 \times 43\%) + (8 \times 21\%) + (8 \times 12\%) + (4 \times 24\%) \\ &= 4.9 \end{aligned} \tag{1.9}$$

Finally, computing the speedup between the results given in Equations 1.8 and 1.9 yields

$$Speedup = \frac{CPI_{real}}{CPI_{perfect}} = \frac{4.9}{1.6} = 3.1$$

Therefore, with a perfect cache the machine is 3.1 times faster than it is with a real cache.

▷ Exercise 1.7

The parts of this exercise explore MIPS and MFLOPS in order to illustrate how they can sometimes be misleading. Throughout Exercises 1.7(a)–1.7(c) we use two of the expressions for MIPS developed in Section 1.8 of the text. The first expression relates MIPS to the clock rate and CPI:

$$MIPS = \frac{Clock\ Rate}{CPI \times 10^6} \tag{1.10}$$

The second expression is simply a different form of Equation 1.10 that relates the instruction count to the execution time and MIPS rating:

$$Instruction\ Count = (Execution\ Time) \times MIPS \times 10^6 \tag{1.11}$$

Finally, Exercise 1.7(d) explores the MFLOPS rating of the Whetstone program. This exercise uses the expression for MFLOPS developed in Section 1.8:

$$MFLOPS = \frac{Number\ of\ FP\ Operations\ in\ the\ Program}{(Execution\ Time\ in\ Seconds) \times 10^6} \tag{1.12}$$

▷ **Exercise 1.7(a)**

For a version of Whetstone that computes its floating point in software, Equation 1.10 yields

$$MIPS_{software} = \frac{16.67 \times 10^6}{6.0 \times 10^6} = 2.8$$

And if the floating point is computed by a coprocessor,

$$MIPS_{coprocessor} = \frac{16.67 \times 10^6}{10.0 \times 10^6} = 1.7$$

Note that the MIPS for the software is almost twice the MIPS for the co-processor even though the execution time for the software is nearly an *order of magnitude* higher! The moral of this exercise is, MIPS actually stands for "Meaningless Indicator of Processor Speed."

▷ **Exercise 1.7(d)**

Using Equation 1.12 in conjunction with the information from the text on Whetstone leads to

$$MFLOPS = \frac{195,578}{1.08 \times 10^6} = 0.18$$

Thus, Whetstone has an MFLOPS rating of 0.18. Because some floating-point operations are more difficult to perform than others, we sometimes weight, or normalize, floating-point operations according to their difficulty by considering "difficult" operations as multiple floating-point operations. Doing so gives a program that executes n "difficult" floating-point operations a higher MFLOPS rating than a program that executes n "easy" operations. In this exercise we weight all operations equally.

▷ **Exercise 1.8**

This group of exercises use the fabrication equations presented in Section 1.4 of the text to explore the yields and costs of various microprocessors. These exercises illustrate how each of the terms in the fabrication equations contribute to the total cost of a complete IC. To solve these exercises, a subset of the equations outlined in this discussion is applied to the information given in the exercise statement.

The first parameter we generally compute is the number of square die that can be placed onto a round wafer, *Die per Wafer*, which is given by the following relationship between wafer diameter and die area:

$$Die\ per\ Wafer = \left\lfloor \frac{\pi\left(\frac{1}{2} Wafer\ Diam.\right)^2}{Die\ Area} - \frac{\pi\left(Wafer\ Diam.\right)}{\sqrt{2\left(Die\ Area\right)}} \right\rfloor \qquad (1.13)$$

Because die come in integral quantities, we take the floor[1] of the right-hand side of this equation. Also of interest is the percentage of die on a wafer that are free from manufacturing defects, *Die Yield*, given by

$$Die\ Yield = \left(Wafer\ Yield\right)\left[1 + \frac{\left(Defects\ per\ Area\right)\left(Die\ Area\right)}{\alpha}\right]^{-\alpha} \qquad (1.14)$$

The die yield is controlled by the defect density, die area, and the parameter α, which describes the "complexity" of the manufacturing process. Multiplying Equations 1.14 and 1.13 together provides the number of good die per wafer:

$$Good\ Die\ per\ Wafer = \lfloor Die\ per\ Wafer \times Die\ Yield \rfloor \qquad (1.15)$$

Again, given that die come in integral quantities we take the floor in this equation. Exercise 1.8(a) utilizes this equation to find the number of good die per wafer for several recent microprocessors.

Given the number of die per wafer, a die yield, and a wafer cost, we can find the cost of untested and unpackaged die from

$$Die\ Cost = \frac{Wafer\ Cost}{Good\ Die\ per\ Wafer} = \frac{Wafer\ Cost}{\lfloor Die\ per\ Wafer \times Die\ Yield \rfloor} \qquad (1.16)$$

The yield appears in the denominator because the good die must pay for the bad die. Exercise 1.8(b) utilizes this equation to find the cost of a die for a group of microprocessors.

In addition to the cost of an unpackaged and untested die, the die yield can be used to determine the cost to test the die:

$$Testing\ Cost = \frac{Cost\ per\ Unit\ Time \times Testing\ Time}{Die\ Yield} \qquad (1.17)$$

The terms in the numerator depend on the type of testing equipment that is required and the amount of time required to test each die.

---

[1] We define the floor of x, written $\lfloor x \rfloor$, as the largest integer y such that $y \leq x$.

Microprocessor	Die per Wafer	Die Yield	Good Die per Wafer
MIPS 4600	357	0.48	171
PowerPC 603	321	0.45	144
HP 71x0	128	0.21	26
Digital 21064a	154	0.26	40
SuperSPARC/60	94	0.15	14

Figure 1.4: Number of Good Die per Wafer for Several Microprocessors.

Finally, the die cost from Equation 1.16 along with the testing cost from Equation 1.17, combined with information on the cost of packaging, allows the total cost of a tested and packaged IC to be determined.

$$IC\ Cost = \frac{Die\ Cost + Testing\ Cost + Packaging\ Cost}{Final\ Test\ Yield} \qquad (1.18)$$

states that the cost of an IC is given by the sum of the various costs associated with producing the IC divided by the yield (or, the percentage of die that make it through the production process). The cost terms are divided by the final yield, as the good die must shoulder the costs of die that fail along the way. Exercises 1.8(c), 1.8(d), and 1.8(e) utilize this equation to find the total cost of various die.

▷ Exercise 1.8(a)

Given the fabrication equations outlined in the above introduction, this exercise is solved simply by plugging the information from the exercise statement into Equation 1.15 assuming a 20cm wafer, a defect density of $1cm^{-2}$, an α of 3, and a wafer yield of 95%. Doing the math yields the number of good die per wafer shown in Figure 1.4 for the microprocessors we are exploring. As expected, the smaller die have better yields. This affects the cost of a completed device, as we shall see shortly. Remember to be wary of the units of each quantity when computing these results (the exercise provides die area in mm^2 and defect density in cm^{-2}, for example).

▷ Exercise 1.8(e)

Finding the total cost of a Digital 21064a microprocessor requires three steps that use the fabrication equations discussed above in addition to the information in Figures 1.22 and 1.23 of the text:

α	Die per Wafer	Die Yield	Die Cost	Testing Cost	IC Cost
3.0	154	0.33	$80.00	$3.90	$133.90
4.5	154	0.31	$83.80	$4.20	$138.00

Figure 1.5: Costs of a Digital 21064a Microprocessor for Two Different Defect Densities.

1. Solve Equation 1.15 for the number of good die per wafer, assuming a 20cm wafer, a defect density of $0.8\mathrm{cm}^{-2}$, the values of α given in the exercise statement, and a wafer yield of 95%.

2. Use the values from Step 1 to solve Equation 1.16 for the cost of an unpackaged, untested die assuming the wafer costs given in the exercise statement.

3. Use the values from Step 2 to solve Equation 1.18 for the total cost using assumptions on testing time and packaging costs given in the exercise statement and assuming the final test yield is 100%.

These steps are repeated for the two alphas specified in the exercise statement, 3 and 4.5.

For either value of α, Equation 1.13 implies that 154 Digital 21064a die fit on each 20cm wafer. Also, from the exercise statement the packaging costs for a Digital 21064a are $50.00 per die. The die cost and testing cost can then be determined from the information in the exercise statement and Equations 1.16 and 1.17, respectively. Summarizing the results leads to Figure 1.5. A fully tested, packaged Digital 21064a microprocessor costs $133.90 and $138.00 for α values of 3 and 4.5, respectively.

The total cost is not as sensitive to changes in α as it is to changes in defect density (see Exercise 1.8(d)). Increasing α by 50% only increases the total cost by 4%. This implies that adding complexity to a process may be worth the effort as increasing the number of interconnection layers, for example, can decrease the size of the die and thus improve speed (in reality things are not quite this simple, as the layer n of interconnection may not be as fast as layer 1).

▷ Exercise 1.9

The solution to this exercise can be derived by setting the squares of the expressions for the arithmetic mean and the geometric mean equal and solving:

$$\left(\frac{a+b}{2}\right)^2 = \left(\sqrt{a \times b}\right)^2$$

Multiplying and solving yields

$$(a - b)^2 = 0$$

which implies the geometric mean and arithmetic mean are equal only when $a = b$.

To show that the arithmetic mean is always greater than or equal to the geometric mean, we first note the following lemma for any positive x and y.

Lemma 1 *If $x^2 - y^2 \geq 0$, then $x^2 \geq y^2$ and $x \geq y$.*

Therefore,

$$
\begin{aligned}
\left(\frac{a+b}{2}\right)^2 - ab &= \frac{a^2 + 2ab + b^2}{4} - \frac{4ab}{4} \\
&= \frac{a^2 - 2ab + b^2}{4} \\
&= \frac{(a-b)^2}{4} \geq 0
\end{aligned}
$$

and so

$$\left(\frac{a+b}{2}\right)^2 - ab \geq 0$$

which implies

$$\frac{a+b}{2} \geq \sqrt{ab}$$

This shows that the arithmetic mean is always greater than or equal to the geometric mean.

▷ Exercise 1.11

This question uses the SPEC data from Figure 1.24 in the text to compare how weighted means can be calculated and used and how they compare to the geometric means given in Figure 1.24 of the text.

Benchmark	Weight
spice2g6	0.0176
doduc	0.2208
mdljdp2	0.0595
wave5	0.1143
tomcatv	0.1592
ora	0.0569
alvinn	0.0549
ear	0.0165
mdljsp2	0.1260
swm256	0.0332
su2cor	0.0327
hydro2d	0.0308
nasa7	0.0251
fpppp	0.0459

Figure 1.6: Weights Required to Ensure Equal Running Times on a VAX-11/780.

▷ **Exercise 1.11(a)**

To solve this exercise, we can apply the equation provided in Section 1.5 of the text:

$$Weight_i = \frac{1}{Time_i \times \sum_{j=1}^{N} \frac{1}{Time_j}} \tag{1.19}$$

Computing the value of the summation term for the VAX times yields

$$\sum_{j=1}^{N} \frac{1}{Time_j} = 0.00237$$

Now, applying Equation 1.19 to each of the times for the VAX 11/780 yields the weights shown in Figure 1.6.

▷ **Exercise 1.12**

To solve these exercises, we first have to develop a new and improved form of Amdahl's Law that can handle multiple enhancements without serious gastrointestinal disorder. The key feature of these exercises that makes extending Amdahl's Law straightforward is the fact that only one enhancement can be used at a time. If you recall from the text (and if you do not you should go back and read the section on Amdahl's Law this instant), Amdahl's Law is formed by computing the speedup for the fraction of time an enhancement can be used and adding to that the fraction of time the system is not running in the enhanced mode.

As only one enhancement can be used at any point in time, we can derive a form of Amdahl's Law that allows for several enhancements. Basically, we extend Amdahl's Law by changing the terms involving the fraction of time an enhancement can be used into summations:

$$Speedup = \left[\left(1 - \sum_i FE_i\right) + \sum_i \frac{FE_i}{SE_i}\right]^{-1} \tag{1.20}$$

where FE_i is the fraction of time enhancement i could be used in the unoptimized system, and SE_i is the speedup from enhancement i. Equation 1.20 reduces to the familiar form of Amdahl's Law when there is a single enhancement. This form of Amdahl's Law only works if the enhancements are non-overlapping. That is, at most *one* enhancement is usable at any point in time. The terms in Equation 1.20 directly correspond to the terms in the version of Amdahl's Law discussed in the text—the first term represents the amount of time no enhancement is usable, and the remaining terms represent the time spent using the enhancements.

▷ Exercise 1.12(a)

To solve this exercise, we need to find the fraction of time the third enhancement must be used to ensure a speedup of 10. Plugging the appropriate values into the new and improved version of Amdahl's Law developed above in Equation 1.20 and solving for the fraction of time the third enhancement is in use, FE_3, gives

$$
\begin{aligned}
Speedup &= \left\{[1 - (FE_1 + FE_2 + FE_3)] + \frac{FE_1}{SE_1} + \frac{FE_2}{SE_2} + \frac{FE_3}{SE_3}\right\}^{-1} \\
10 &= \left\{[1 - (0.30 + 0.30 + FE_3)] + \frac{0.30}{30} + \frac{0.30}{20} + \frac{FE_3}{10}\right\}^{-1} \\
0.10 &= 0.425 + \left(\frac{1}{10} - 1\right) FE_3 \\
&\Rightarrow FE_3 = 0.36
\end{aligned}
$$

Therefore, the third enhancement must be usable in the unenhanced system 36% of the time to achieve an overall speedup of 10.

▷ Exercise 1.13

This question shows how using the MIPS rating of a computer system instead of a comparison of execution time can yield results that do not correlate.

▷ Exercise 1.13(a)

To write the formula for MIPS, we need to compute the total number of instructions executed and the time that it took to execute them. Once this has been done, we can use the general equation

$$MIPS = \frac{Instruction\ Count}{Execution\ Time \times 10^6}$$

For the configuration without the coprocessor, the total instruction count is the number of integer instructions plus the number of floating-point instructions times the number of integer instructions required to execute each floating-point instruction: $I + F \times Y$. The time to execute the code is given as W seconds.

$$MIPS = \frac{I + F \times Y}{W \times 10^6} \tag{1.21}$$

For the configuration with the coprocessor, the total instruction count is the number of integer instructions plus the number of floating-point operations: $I + F$. The time to execute the code is given as B seconds.

$$MIPS = \frac{I + F}{B \times 10^6} \tag{1.22}$$

▷ Exercise 1.13(b)

To find the value of I for the workstation without the coprocessor, we can use Equation 1.21 derived in Exercise 1.13(a):

$$MIPS = \frac{I + F \times Y}{W \times 10^6}$$

Plugging in the known values from the exercise statement yields

$$120 = \frac{I + (8 \times 10^6) \times 50}{4 \times 10^6}$$

Solving for I yields a result of

$$I = 8 \times 10^7$$

Prog.	Computer A		Computer B		Computer C	
	Time	MFLOPS	Time	MFLOPS	Time	MFLOPS
P1	1	100	10	10	20	5
P2	1000	0.1	100	1	20	5
Total	1001	—	110	—	40	—

Figure 1.7: The MFLOPS Ratings of Two Programs Running on Three Computers.

▷ Exercise 1.14

These exercises examine the applications of the arithmetic, harmonic, and geometric means to summarizing MFLOPS information.

▷ Exercise 1.14(a)

Recall the equation for MFLOPS presented in Section 1.8 of the text:

$$MFLOPS = \frac{Number\ of\ Floating - Point\ Operations\ in\ a\ Program}{(Execution\ Time\ in\ Seconds) \times 10^6}$$

(1.23)

As MFLOPS represents millions of floating-point operations per second, Equation 1.23 should make sense—MFLOPS is just the number of floating-point operations divided by time.

To solve this exercise, all we do is plug the execution times given in Figure 1.11 of the text and the number of floating-point operations per program specified in the exercise statement into Equation 1.23. Figure 1.7 shows the execution times (in seconds) and the MFLOPS ratings achieved by programs P1 and P2 when they are run on computers A, B, and C. In addition, the total execution time of both programs is shown for each computer.

▷ Exercise 1.15

This exercise shows how using normalized FLOPS instead of native FLOPS can impact the rated MFLOPS of a system. We are asked to compare the results for the DECstation 3100 running spice by using both normalized and native FLOPS. Recall the equation for MFLOPS presented in Section 1.8 of the text:

$$MFLOPS = \frac{Number \ of \ FloatingPoint \ Operations \ in \ a \ Program}{(Execution \ Time \ in \ Seconds) \times 10^6} \quad (1.24)$$

▷ Exercise 1.15(a)

To compute the native MFLOPS rating of the DECstation 3100 running `spice`, we simply apply the standard formula for MFLOPS discussed above. We are given that `spice` runs in 94 seconds and that there are a total of $109,970,178$ FLOPs listed in Figure 1.26 of the text. Plugging these values into Equation 1.24 for MFLOPS yields

$$MFLOPS = \frac{109,970,178}{94 \times 10^6} = 1.17$$

Thus a DECstation running `spice` achieves 1.17 MFLOPS.

Chapter 2

Instruction Set Principles and Examples

Introduction to the Chapter 2 Exercises

With the preliminaries taken care of in Chapter 1, we next turn our attention to actual computer architecture. Chapter 2 of the text focuses on the portion of the architecture visible to the programmer: the instruction set. After discussing the strengths and weaknesses of several common instruction set styles the text examines how to implement an instruction set by covering issues such as encoding the operands. Additionally, the compiler is considered in order to explore some of the issues that cut across hardware and software boundaries. Finally, the chapter concludes with a discussion of DLX, a MIPS-esque load/store instruction set that is used throughout the remainder of the text as the instruction set realized by the various architectures the text explores.

▷ Exercise 2.1

This exercise compares the trade-offs between using various fixed-length fields in offsets for branch and memory instructions and analyze their impact on the overall size of programs. For these exercises, we use the average instruction length as our measurement of choice. The average instruction length is computed by summing over all instruction lengths the product of a length and the percentage of instructions having this length.

▷ **Exercise 2.1(a)**

For this question, we are given execution profiles in Figure 2.32 of the text that describe how many offset instruction bits are needed for various instructions. Armed with this information, we are asked to decide what the average instruction length (*AIL*) would be if there were three formats for instructions based on the number of bits required for the offset field (rounded to the nearest byte).

To make answering this type of question easier, it is best to break them into smaller pieces. We note that a simple formula for computing the average instruction length is

$$AIL = (Percent_0 \times 16) + (Percent_8 \times 24) + (Percent_{16} \times 32) \qquad (2.1)$$

where $Percent_x$ is the percentage of instructions that require x bits for the offset field. To compute the individual terms in Equation 2.1, we start by summarizing some of the important data gathered from the tables:

1. Loads and stores constitute 35% of the instructions and

   (a) 17% require 0 offset bits
   (b) 43% require between 1 and 8 offset bits
   (c) 40% require between 9 and 16 offset bits

2. Branches and jumps constitute 19% of the instructions and

   (a) 0% require 0 offset bits
   (b) 98% require between 1 and 8 offset bits
   (c) 2% require between 9 and 16 offset bits

3. The remaining instructions (assumed to be ALU operations) constitute 46% of the instructions and require no offset bits.

To compute $Percent_0$, the percentage of instructions that require no extra offset bits, we compute the portion of instructions of each type that can run with no offset bits:

$$Percent_0 = (0.17 \times 35\%) + (0.00 \times 19\%) + (46\%) = 52\%$$

for $Percent_8$:

$$Percent_8 = (0.43 \times 35\%) + (0.98 \times 19\%) = 34\%$$

and finally for $Percent_{16}$:

$$Percent_{16} = (0.40 \times 35\%) + (0.02 \times 19\%) = 14\%$$

Now that we have computed the the percentage of instructions that require specific offset values, we can just plug the result into Equation 2.1:

$$
\begin{aligned}
AIL &= (Percent_0 \times 16) + (Percent_8 \times 24) + (Percent_{16} \times 32) \\
&= 21 \; bits
\end{aligned}
$$

▷ Exercise 2.2

This question asks you to analyze the trade-offs between adding a new instruction to a load-store architecture that decreases the number of instructions executed at the cost of increasing the overall clock cycle by 10%.

▷ Exercise 2.2(a)

Keep in mind that because the new design has a clock cycle time equal to 1.10 times the old clock cycle time, the new design must execute fewer instructions to achieve the same execution time. Once again we find ourselves using our old friend CPU time to solve this exercise:

$$
\begin{aligned}
CPU \; Time &= CPI \times (Clock \; Cycle \; Time) \times (Instruction \; Count) \\
&= CPI \times Clk \times IC
\end{aligned}
$$

For the original configuration, this equation yields

$$CPU \; Time_{old} = CPI_{old} \times Clk_{old} \times IC_{old} \tag{2.2}$$

and for the modified configuration:

$$
\begin{aligned}
CPU \; Time_{new} &= CPI_{new} \times Clk_{new} \times IC_{new} \\
&= CPI_{old} \times (1.10 \times Clk_{old}) \times (IC_{old} - R) \tag{2.3}
\end{aligned}
$$

In Equation 2.3, we assume that the CPI of the new configuration is equal to that of the old (as indicated in the exercise statement), the new clock cycle time is 10% longer than the old configuration, and the new configuration executes R fewer instructions than the old (due to the optimization).

```
for (i=0; i<=100; i++) {
    A[i] = B[i] + C;
}
```

Figure 2.1: Original C Loop.

To find out how many loads must be removed to achieve the same performance, set Equations 2.2 and 2.3 equal and solve for the ratio of instruction counts:

$$CPI_{old} \times Clk_{old} \times IC_{old} = CPI_{old} \times (1.10 \times Clk_{old}) \times (IC_{old} - R)$$
$$\frac{IC_{old} - R}{IC_{old}} = 0.91$$

solving for R yields 0.09. Thus, 9% of all instructions must be removed to get the same performance (this 9% is completely composed of loads). Because loads account for 22.8% of the instruction mix of **gcc** from Figure 2.26, 39.5% (computed from $\frac{9\%}{22.8\%} = 39.5\%$) of the loads must be replaced with the new load/operation combined instruction for the performance of the old and new configurations to be the same.

Introduction to Exercises 2.6–2.9

These exercises ask us to write machine code for the simple C loop shown in Figure 2.1. After writing the machine code for this loop, we compute the number of instructions executed, the number of data references, and the program size in bytes for the machine code. The machine code is written in both optimized and unoptimized forms for both the DLX and 80x86 architectures (see Appendix E for more information on the 80x86).

The intent of these exercises is to illustrate how architecture and compiler optimizations can influence the instructions executed. It is very informative to compare the results not only within the various machine architectures, but also between the DLX and 80x86.

▷ Exercise 2.6

Because this question states not to use register reuse for the values of variables, we must load them from memory each time they are read, and the

```
ex2_6:
            ADDI    R1, R0, #1        ; initialize i
            SW      2000(R0), R1      ; store 1

loop:
            LW      R1, 2000(R0)      ; get value of i
            MULT    R2, R1, #4        ; R2 = word offset of B
            ADDI    R3, R2, #5000     ; add base address to R2

            LW      R4,    0(R3)      ; LD value of B[i]
            LW      R5, 1500(R0)      ; LD value of C

            ADD     R6, R4, R5        ; B[i] + C

            LW      R1, 2000(R0)      ; get value of i
            MULT    R2, R1, #4        ; R2 = word offset of A
            ADDI    R7, R2, #0        ; add base address to R2
            SW      0(R7), R6         ; A[i] <- B[i] + C

            LW      R1, 2000(R0)      ; get value of i
            ADDI    R1, R1, #1        ; increment i
            SW      2000(R0), R1      ; store i

            LW      R1, 2000(R0)      ; get value of i
            ADDI    R8, R1, #-101     ; is counter at 101?
            BNEZ    R8, loop          ; if not 101, repeat
```

Figure 2.2: Naive DLX Machine Code to Implement the C Loop.

value must be stored back to its location after each update. Also, because the addresses of all the variables are less than 16 bits, we can use immediate instructions to load their addresses. The DLX code in Figure 2.2 shows one possible translation of the C code in Figure 2.1. There are many ways to improve this code, but none were performed because the point of the question is to expose the value of compiler optimizations (see Exercise 2.8).

The total number of instructions executed is the number of setup instructions plus the number of instructions in the loop times the number of iterations:

$$Instructions\ Executed = 2 + (16 \times 101) = 1618$$

To compute the total number of data references executed, we add the number of data references per iteration multiplied by the number of iterations to the number of data references in the setup code:

$$Data\ References\ Executed = 1 + (8 \times 101) = 809$$

The code size is just the total number of instructions in the assembly program times 4 (since there are 4 bytes per instruction in DLX):

$$Instruction\ Bytes = 4 \times 18 = 72$$

▷ Exercise 2.9

To generate the code required for this exercise, we take the same approach used in Exercise 2.8 for DLX. Namely, we optimize the 80x86 code and assume that values can be carried in registers between loop iterations. The 80x86 code in Figure 2.3 shows one possible translation of the C code in Figure 2.1 using simple optimizations. In this code, we assume that the various segment registers and such are initialized prior to entry. If we weren't concerned about saving the loop index, i, we could replace the **inc**, **cmp**, and **jne** instructions with a **loop** instruction and iterate the loop backwards from 101 to 1. This would reduce the code in the loop to *four* instructions. Although the code is very compact, 80x86 instructions are much more difficult to efficiently pipeline than DLX instructions.

When executing, the five instructions starting at **ex2_9** each execute once, while the six instructions in the loop body, which begins at **qux**, execute one hundred times and the termination instruction at **reap** executes once. Thus, the dynamic instruction count is

$$Instructions\ Executed = 5 + (6 \times 101) + 1 = 612$$

The initialization code before **qux** makes a single memory access (the **mov** **%ebx,[1500]** being the guilty party), the **lodsl** and **stosl** instructions each make one access in the loop body, and the instruction at **reap** also makes a single memory access. Therefore, the number of data references is

$$Data\ References\ Executed = 1 + (2 \times 101) + 1 = 204$$

Finally, this code is 12 instructions long and 27 bytes long.

```
ex2_9:
            mov     %ecx, #1        ; initialize i to 1
            lea     %edi, 4         ; load address or A[1]
            lea     %esi, 2004      ; load address of B[1]
            mov     %ebx, [1500]    ; load ebx with C
            cld                     ; make lods/stos incr.

    qux:
            lodsl                   ; load B[i] and
                                    ; increment B[i] ptr
            addl    %eax, %ebx      ; compute B[i] + C
            stosl                   ; A[i] = B[i] + C and
                                    ; increment A[i] ptr

            incl    %ecx            ; increment i

            cmpl    %ecx, #101      ; is i at 101 yet?
            jne     qux             ; if not, back to qux

    reap:
            movl    [2000], %ecx    ; save final value of i
```

Figure 2.3: Optimized 80x86 Machine Code to Implement the C Loop.

▷ Exercise 2.10

Since this exercise asks for the percentage of various types of memory accesses, we will need the following formulae:

$$Percent_{data\ access} = \frac{Number_{data\ access}}{Number_{memory\ access}}$$

$$Percent_{data\ read} = \frac{Number_{data\ read}}{Number_{data\ access}}$$

$$Percent_{memory\ read} = \frac{Number_{memory\ read}}{Number_{memory\ access}}$$

where $Percent_{data\ access}$ is the percentage of memory accesses that are for data, $Percent_{data\ read}$ is the percentage of data accesses that are reads, and $Percent_{memory\ read}$ is the percentage of all memory accesses that are reads.

To solve the above equations, we need to compute the unknowns on the right-hand side of the equations. These can be computed based on the knowledge that each load is one data read, each store is one data write, and each instruction executed is one memory read. The equations below use this information along with the fact that 26% of the instructions are loads and 9% of the instructions are stores (from Figure 2.26 in the text).

$$Number_{memory\ access} = Number_{instructions} \times (1 + 0.26 + 0.09)$$
$$Number_{data\ access} = Number_{instructions} \times (0.26 + 0.09)$$
$$Number_{data\ read} = Number_{instructions} \times (0.26)$$
$$Number_{memory\ read} = Number_{instructions} \times (1 + 0.26)$$

Notice that $Number_{instructions}$ is a term in all of the $Number_i$ equations above and thus it will drop out when plugged in to the $Percent_i$ ratios above.

Plugging the $Number_i$ equations above into the $Percent_i$ ratios above yields

$$Percent_{data\ access} = 26\%$$
$$Percent_{data\ read} = 74\%$$
$$Percent_{memory\ read} = 93\%$$

▷ Exercise 2.12

This exercise provides an excellent example of how a computer architect might go about analyzing the potential performance impact of a new architectural feature. It explores adding a new addressing mode, which, in some cases, reduces the number of instructions required to perform a common operation. The change allows us to perform loads and stores that have an effective address specified by the sum of two registers and a constant. The first part of the exercise requires us to evaluate the change in instruction count and the second part examine the potential speedup of the modification.

▷ Exercise 2.12(a)

Our first task in solving this exercise is to determine what percentage of instructions are able to take advantage of the new addressing mode. Before going on it is helpful to describe *exactly* how the modification changes the instruction count. Consider the code fragment written for the unmodified version of DLX, or "Classic DLX," shown in Figure 2.4. Essentially, the first **add** instruction is used to compute part of the effective address used

```
scsi:    add      r1,r1,r2        ; r1 = r1 + r2
         lw       r4,0(r1)        ; load from 0 + r1
```

Figure 2.4: Code Sequence on "Classic DLX."

```
vram:    lw       r4,0(r1,r2)     ; load from 0 + r1 + r2
```

Figure 2.5: The Same Code Sequence for "New DLX."

in a later load or store instruction. On the modified version of DLX, or "New DLX," the code fragment shown in Figure 2.4 would be modified to read as in Figure 2.5. In this code, the **add** has been folded into the load or store instruction by using some of the bits in the constant offset to encode a register instead (we can view this modification as either removing the load/store *or* removing the add).

The exercise statement informs us that 10% of the displacement loads and stores can use the new addressing mode (note that this number accounts for both the type of address calculation and the shorter offset). From Figure 2.26 of the text, displacement loads and stores constitute 26% and 9%, respectively, of the instruction mix for the five SPECint92 programs. In the optimized version of the architecture, the add that is paired with 10% of the displacement loads or stores can be removed. Such adds constitute 3.5% of the instruction mix $((10\% \times 26\%) + (10\% \times 9\%))$ and are not executed by New DLX with the additional addressing mode. Thus, assuming Classic DLX executes $IC_{classic}$ instructions, the percentage of these instructions executed on New DLX is

$$\frac{IC_{new}}{IC_{classic}} = \frac{IC_{classic} - IC_{classic}\left[(10\% \times 26\%) + (10\% \times 9\%)\right]}{IC_{classic}}$$

$$= \frac{0.965\,(IC_{classic})}{IC_{classic}} = 0.965 \tag{2.4}$$

New DLX with its additional addressing mode executes 96.5% of the instructions executed by Classic DLX.

Chapter 3

Pipelining

Introduction to the Chapter 3 Exercises

With the advent of the DLX instruction set in Chapter 2, the text moves on to consider how we might build a machine that implements this instruction set. Chapter 3 focuses on the basic issues relating to pipelining. The discussion covers hazards and their impact on the pipeline, the issues that make life difficult for a pipeline designer, how multicycle operations can be handled in the context of pipelining, and how the choice of instruction set can help or hinder the design of a pipeline. The chapter concludes with a study of the MIPS R4000 pipeline that serves to illustrate many of the concepts discussed in the chapter in the context of a real processor.

Throughout the solutions in this chapter, we sometimes use single letter abbreviations in the pipeline diagrams to represent the pipeline stages. For the standard five-stage DLX pipeline "F" corresponds to "IF," "D" corresponds to "ID," "X" corresponds to "EX," "M" corresponds to "MEM," "W" corresponds to "WB," and "s" corresponds to a stall. Finally, many of these exercises have a number of reasonable solutions that could be derived depending on the assumptions made.

▷ Exercise 3.1

This exercise leaves some aspects, of the pipeline undefined (e.g., where in the pipeline branches resolve). As any of several reasonable assumptions can be made about such aspects, answers to this exercise may differ from that presented here.

These questions involve showing how a given code sequence performs given a series of different assumptions about available pipeline bypassing, register forwarding, and branch implementation.

It should be apparent from the information on the code fragment given in the exercise statement that the loop iterates 99 times. With this data point, we can determine how many cycles the loop takes to complete by examining a pipeline diagram such as Figure 3.14 in the text. In the pipeline diagram we look for the length of iterations 0 through 97 and add in the length of the last iteration. The first 98 iterations should be of the same length.

▷ Exercise 3.1(a)

To answer this question only requires that we go through one complete iteration of the loop and the first instruction in the next iteration. The pipeline diagram for this exercise is shown in Figure 3.1. There are several cycles lost to stalls in this figure:

- *Cycles 3–4:* addi stalls ID to wait for lw to write back r1.

- *Cycles 6–7:* sw stalls ID to wait for addi to write back r1.

- *Cycles 10–11:* sub stalls ID to wait for addi to write back r2.

- *Cycles 13–14:* bnz stalls ID to wait for sub to write back r4.

- *Cycles 16–17:* bnz computes the next PC in MEM implying that the lw can not be fetched until after cycle 17 (note the fetch in cycle 15 is also wasted).

In this figure we have assumed the version of DLX described in Figure 3.21 in the text, which resolves branches in MEM. Figure 3.1 changes slightly if we use the version of DLX specified in Figure 3.23 of the text which resolves branches in ID.

From Figure 3.1 the second iteration begins 17 clocks after the first iteration and the last iteration takes 18 cycles to complete. This implies that iteration i (where iterations are numbered from 0 to 98) begins on clock cycle $1 + (i \times 17)$. As the loop executes 99 times the loop executes in a total of $(98 \times 17) + 18 = 1684$ clocks.

Instruction	Clock Cycle																					
	1	2	3	4	5	6	7	8	9	10	11	12	13	14	15	16	17	18	19	20	21	22
lw r1,0(r2)	F	D	X	M	W																	
addi r1,r1,#1		F	s	s	D	X	M	W														
sw r1,0(r2)				F	s	s	D	X	M	W												
addi r2,r2,#4						F	D	X	M	W												
sub r4,r3,r2							F	s	s	D	X	M	W									
bnz r4,loop									F	s	s	D	X	M	W							
lw r1,0(r2)												F	s	s	F	D	X	M	W			

Figure 3.1: Pipeline Diagram for an Unbypassed DLX Pipeline Executing the Integer Loop.

▷ Exercise 3.2

> *This exercise leaves some aspects of the pipeline undefined (e.g., where in the pipeline branches resolve). As any of several reasonable assumptions can be made about such aspects, answers to this exercise may differ from that presented here.*

The performance of a pipeline is heavily dependent on both hardware, such as forwarding or bypassing paths, and software, such as code scheduling, features. In these exercises, we explore how the performance of a small FP loop on DLX changes as we improve the bypassing and code scheduling.

It should be apparent from the information on the code fragment given in the exercise statement that the loop iterates 99 times. With this data point, we can determine how many cycles the loop takes to complete by examining a pipeline diagram such as Figure 3.14 in the text. In the pipeline diagram we look for the length of iterations 0 through 97 and add in the length of the last iteration. The first 98 iterations should be of the same length.

▷ Exercise 3.2(c)

Our first task in solving this exercise is to schedule the code from the exercise to remove as many stalls as possible. To schedule the code, you should attempt to ensure that any instruction i using a result of an instruction j does not issue before the latency of instruction j has been satisfied. Also, any code movement must not disturb the function of the program. One possible schedule of the code is shown in Figure 3.2. For example, in Figure 3.2 the

```
loop:    ld      f0,0(r2)        ; load A[i]
         ld      f4,0(r3)        ; load B[i]
         addi    r2,r2,#8        ; bump A[i] pointer
         multd   f0,f0,f4        ; compute A[i] * B[i]
         sub     r5,r4,r2        ; loop term. test...
         addd    f2,f0,f2        ; compute S + A[i]*B[i]
         bnz     r5,loop         ; go back if not done
         addi    r3,r3,#8        ; bump B[i] pointer
```

Figure 3.2: Scheduled DLX FP Loop.

addi has been moved between the second ld and the multd. This change was made because the multd requires the result of the second ld, which has a latency of one (using the definition of latency on page 189 in Section 3.7 of the text). The movement of the addi allows useful work to take place during the latency of the second ld. It is important to notice that the relative ordering between the addi and instructions that use r2 (which the addi modifies) has been preserved in the scheduled code.

With the scheduled code, we can develop a pipeline diagram that shows the first iteration and a portion of the second for the scheduled code running on a DLX with normal bypassing. Such a pipeline diagram is presented in Figure 3.3. There are several stalls in this diagram:

- *Cycles 8–12:* addd stalls EX to wait for multd to forward f0.

- *Cycle 16:* ld stalls EX to avoid contention with addd for the MEM and WB stages of the pipeline.

By scheduling the code and using bypassing, we have eliminated most of the stalls found in Exercises 3.2(a) and 3.2(b).

If you look carefully at Figure 3.3 you should see that the state of the pipeline at cycle 17 is similar to the state in cycle 3 (while the addd and addi are still in the pipe, they can not stall any instructions issuing after cycle 17). Thus, each iteration requires fourteen cycles. Also, two cycles are spent entering the repeating section as the section does not begin until cycle 3. Finally, two cycles are spent leaving because on the final iteration, the addd and addi instructions do not complete until two cycles after the repetition has ended. Therefore, the scheduled version of the loop requires $2 + (14 \times 99) + 2 = 1390$ cycles to execute.

Instruction	Clock Cycle																		
	1	2	3	4	5	6	7	8	9	10	11	12	13	14	15	16	17	18	19
ld f0,0(r2)	F	D	X	M	W														
ld f4,0(r3)		F	D	X	M	W													
addi r2,r2,#8			F	D	X	M	W												
multd f0,f0,f4				F	D	X	X	X	X	X	X	X	M	W					
sub r5,r4,r2					F	D	X	M	W										
addd f2,f0,f2						F	D	s	s	s	s	s	X	X	X	X	M	W	
bnz r5,loop							F	s	s	s	s	s	D	X	M	W			
addi r3,r3,#8													F	D	X	M	W		
ld f0,0(r2)														F	D	s	X	M	W
ld f4,0(r3)															F	s	D	X	M
addi r2,r2,#8																F	D	X	

Figure 3.3: Pipeline Diagram for a Fully Bypassed DLX Pipeline Executing a Scheduled Version of the FP Loop.

▷ Exercise 3.3

The pipeline in this exercise is not specified in the detail that the DLX pipeline was earlier in the text. As a result, unless otherwise noted we assume that the function of the various stages is similar to that of the equivalent DLX stages.

This exercise explores how bypassing, forwarding, and interlocking logic need to be added to prevent stalls in a hypothetical pipeline. The pipeline examined is based on the pipeline used in the VAX 8700 but is slightly simplified for our purposes.

▷ Exercise 3.3(a)

To avoid structural hazards we must ensure that any pipe stage that may require an adder has its own. The simplest way to determine how many adders the architecture requires is to consider each pipeline stage in turn:

- IF always requires an adder to increment the PC.

- RF and WB do not require adders because these stages only read from and write to the register file.

```
froboz: add     r3,r4,r5           ; (ALU2) r4 + r5
        nop                        ; (MEM)
        add     r1,r0,0x667(r9)    ; (ALU1) r9 + 0x667
        nop                        ; (RF)
        nop                        ; (IF) PC + 4
```

Figure 3.4: Code Fragment That Requires the Maximum Number of Adders.

- ALU1 may require an adder to compute the effective address of some memory instructions.

- MEM does not require an adder because it accesses memory and relies on ALU1 to perform any needed address computations.

- ALU2 may use an adder to perform ALU operations required by the instruction.

From this jaunt down the pipeline, we conclude that in the worst case three adders are required (one in each of the IF, ALU1, and ALU2 stages).

For all three adders to be in use during a single cycle, certain types of instructions must be simultaneously in the IF, ALU1, and ALU2 stages:

- IF processes any instruction.

- ALU1 processes a memory access instruction that requires an effective address computation (e.g., add r1,r2,0x10(r3)).

- ALU2 processes an instruction requiring an adder to compute its result (e.g., add r1,r2,r3).

Any code sequence that uses all three adders during a single cycle, such as the code presented in Figure 3.4, must have the above three features. In Figure 3.4 each instruction's comment identifies both the stage the instruction is in during the cycle when all three adders are in use and the function performed by the adder. In this code, nop instructions ("no operation") appear in the MEM, RF, and IF pipe stages where it does not matter what instructions are being processed.

▷ **Exercise 3.3(c)**

To solve the exercise, we must consider whether a condition can arise where a later instruction in the pipeline requires a result produced by an earlier

Instruction	Clock Cycle								
	1	**2**	**3**	**4**	**5**	**6**	**7**	**8**	**9**
i	IF	RF	A1	M	A2	WB			
$i + 1$		IF	RF	A1	M	A2	WB		
$i + 2$			IF	RF	A1	M	A2	WB	
$i + 3$				IF	RF	A1	M	A2	WB
$i + 4$					IF	RF	...		

Figure 3.5: A Pipeline.

instruction that has not been "committed" to processor state. For this exercise, we only need to find the forwarding paths required between the two ALU stages, ALU1 and ALU2. Before going any farther, we should review the function of the ALU1 and ALU2 pipeline stages.

- The ALU1 stage computes the effective address of a memory access. ALU1's result provides the address of the memory access required by the instruction to the MEM stage of the pipeline.

- The ALU2 stage performs any ALU operations required by an instruction. For example, for an **add** instruction it is the ALU2 stage that adds the values of the source registers.

With this information, we can determine the forwarding paths required between the two ALU stages of the pipeline.

The result produced by ALU1 is used only in the MEM stage of the *same* instruction to provide the effective address of the access and is never needed by a different instruction in the machine. Therefore, there is no need for forwarding paths from ALU1 to either ALU2 or ALU1. The result of the ALU2 stage can be used in either ALU2 or ALU1 of a later instruction. As a result, we may have to forward results from ALU2 to either ALU2 or ALU1 of a subsequent instruction if the proper conditions occur. Before discussing these cases further, let us look at Figure 3.5, which presents a diagram of this pipeline with several instructions in flight. This figure uses abbreviated names for each stages to make the figure fit on the page: A1, A2, and M correspond to stages ALU1, ALU2, and MEM, respectively.

From Figure 3.5, it should be clear that hazards can only exist between instruction i and instructions $i + 1$, $i + 2$, and $i + 3$. Instruction i writes its result in WB in the same clock as instruction $i + 4$ reads its operands in RF. Assuming split-phase write/read of the register file, instruction $i + 4$

will always obtain the correct value of a result produced by instruction i. With the groundwork complete, we can consider each potential data hazard outlined above in greater depth.

In our first hazard case, instruction i produces a value in ALU2 that a following ALU instruction requires in ALU2. To get around the potential hazard, we forward the result from ALU2 to future instructions in the pipeline that require the result. Instruction $i + 1$ can receive the value from i if it is forwarded from the WB stage of i to the inputs of ALU2 in cycle 6. Similarly, instructions $i + 2$ and $i + 3$ can receive the value from i if it is forwarded from the WB stage of i to the source latches for the appropriate register value in cycle 7.

In the second hazardous situation, instruction i produces a value in ALU2 that a following memory operation instruction requires in ALU1. If the consuming instruction is in positions $i + 1$ or $i + 2$, the pipeline must stall because forwarding to $i + 1$ or $i + 2$ requires going back in time (as $i + 1$ and $i + 2$ require the value prior to the beginning of cycle 4, but i does not produce it until the end of cycle 5). Finally, instruction $i + 3$ can receive the value from i if it is forwarded from the WB stage of i to the inputs of ALU1 in cycle 6.

Summarizing the results of the above discussions as per Figure 3.19 in the text leads to Figure 3.6. In this figure the destination of the result can be either ALU input or either latch used to carry the value of the source registers down the pipeline. The phrase "ALU Op" represents any instruction that uses ALU2 to perform a computation, and "EA Op" represents any instruction that computes an effective address. Finally, each line in Figure 3.6 corresponds to two forwarding paths:

1. A path to the "Source 1" input that is activated when the destination register of the source instruction is the same as the source 1 register of the destination instruction.

2. A path to the "Source 2" input that is activated when the destination register of the source instruction is the same as the source 2 register of the destination instruction.

These paths are not explicitly shown to clarify the figure.

▷ Exercise 3.3(e)

In Exercises 3.3(c) and 3.3(d) we have explored the data-forwarding paths required by the pipeline to prevent stalls. Unfortunately, there are several

Source Instruction		Destination Instruction		
Pipeline Register	**Opcode**	**Pipeline Register**	**Opcode**	**Destination of Result**
ALU2/WB	ALU Op	MEM/ALU2	ALU Op	ALU2 Input
ALU2/WB	ALU Op	ALU1/MEM	ALU Op	Source Latch
ALU2/WB	ALU Op	RF/ALU1	ALU Op	Source Latch
ALU2/WB	ALU Op	RF/ALU1	EA Op	ALU1 Input

Figure 3.6: Summary of ALU2/ALU2 and ALU2/ALU1 Forwarding Paths.

cases (identified in these exercises) where a value must be consumed before it is produced to eliminate a hazard. Forwarding can not remove such hazards. Instead, in these cases it is necessary to stall the pipeline with an interlock until the hazard clears. This exercise asks us to identify the interlocks in the pipeline and the number of stall cycles they introduce.

Rather than repeat the discussion from Exercises 3.3(c) and 3.3(d), we state the data hazards that require interlocks:

1. Load instruction i and an instruction $i + 1$ that computes an effective address (ALU1 requires the result from MEM).

2. ALU instruction i and instruction $i + 1$ that computes an effective address (ALU1 requires the result from ALU2).

3. ALU instruction i and store instruction $i + 1$ (MEM requires the result from ALU2).

4. ALU instruction i and instruction $i + 2$ that computes an effective address (ALU1 requires the result from ALU2).

The labeling of instructions (i, $i + 1$, $i + 2$, etc.) indicates the cycle in which they enter the pipeline. These results can be derived by finding each hazard and then determining whether they can be solved with forwarding. Hazards can be found by considering the potential consumers of results produced by the various stages of the pipeline.

At this point, we present the interlock hardware and then briefly discuss how we came up with all this information. For this processor, the interlocking hardware is described in Figure 3.7 as per Figure 3.18 of the text. The phrase "ALU Op" represents any operation that uses ALU2 to perform a computation that includes instructions such as add or compare, and "EA

Case	Opcode #1 In IF/RF Register	Opcode #2	In Pipeline Register	Latency (clocks)
1	EA Op	Load	RF/ALU1	1
2	EA Op	ALU Op	RF/ALU1	2
3	Store	ALU Op	RF/ALU1	1
4	EA Op	ALU Op	ALU1/MEM	1

Figure 3.7: Summary of Pipeline Interlocks.

Op" includes any instruction that requires the computation of an effective address. The interlock is only applied if a source register of Opcode #1 matches the destination register of Opcode #2.

To understand how we arrive at Figure 3.7, let us examine the first case in greater depth. In this case, we are interested in stalling an instruction $i+1$ that computes an effective address, provided instruction i is a load. Now, the opcode in the IF/RF pipeline latch represents the instruction currently in RF. As this is the stage where we like to stall instructions if necessary, we check for the case where instruction $i + 1$ is an "EA Op" here. When instruction $i + 1$ is in the IF/RF pipeline register, instruction i must be in the RF/ALU1 pipeline register as it is a cycle ahead. As a result, we check for an ALU operation in the RF/ALU1 register to determine whether this particular interlock must be enforced. In addition to checking the opcodes, a check must be made to see whether the instruction issuing into the pipe (instruction $i+1$ in this case) uses a register written by the earlier instruction in the pipe (instruction i in this case). The remainder of the cases are determined in a similar fashion.

▷ Exercise 3.7

This solution provides the integer pipeline forwarding logic for ALU, immediate, and load instructions of the R4000. We make the following notes regarding the figure illustrating the forwarding logic:

- Values coming from ALU instructions can be forwarded from any of the stages from EX/DF, DF/DS, DS/TC, or TC/WB as needed by later instructions.

- Loads can come from both the DS/TC and TC/WB stages in the R4000 pipeline since data is available at the end of DS even though

Source Instruction		Destination Instruction		
Pipeline Register	**Opcode**	**Pipeline Register**	**Opcode**	**Destination of Result**
EX/DF	Reg-Reg ALU	RF/EX	Any	ALU Top
EX/DF	Reg-Reg ALU	RF/EX	Reg-Reg ALU	ALU Bottom
DF/DS	Reg-Reg ALU	RF/EX	Any	ALU Top
DF/DS	Reg-Reg ALU	RF/EX	Reg-Reg ALU	ALU Bottom
DS/TC	Reg-Reg ALU	RF/EX	Any	ALU Top
DS/TC	Reg-Reg ALU	RF/EX	Reg-Reg ALU	ALU Bottom
TC/WB	Reg-Reg ALU	RF/EX	Any	ALU Top
TC/WB	Reg-Reg ALU	RF/EX	Reg-Reg ALU	ALU Bottom
EX/DF	ALU-Immed	RF/EX	Any	ALU Top
EX/DF	ALU-Immed	RF/EX	Reg-Reg ALU	ALU Bottom
DF/DS	ALU-Immed	RF/EX	Any	ALU Top
DF/DS	ALU-Immed	RF/EX	Reg-Reg ALU	ALU Bottom
DS/TC	ALU-Immed	RF/EX	Any	ALU Top
DS/TC	ALU-Immed	RF/EX	Reg-Reg ALU	ALU Bottom
TC/WB	ALU-Immed	RF/EX	Any	ALU Top
TC/WB	ALU-Immed	RF/EX	Reg-Reg ALU	ALU Bottom
DS/TC	Load	RF/EX	Any	ALU Top
DS/TC	Load	RF/EX	Reg-Reg ALU	ALU Bottom
TC/WB	Load	RF/EX	Any	ALU Top
TC/WB	Load	RF/EX	Reg-Reg ALU	ALU Bottom

Figure 3.8: R4000 Integer Pipeline Forwarding for ALU, Immediate, and Load Instructions.

the result of the tag match has not been reported.

- We use "Any" as an abbreviation for the description of the following instruction types: Reg-Reg ALU, ALU-Immed, Load, Store, and Branch.

Figure 3.8 shows the complete set of forwarding logic required for this exercise. In each case in this figure it is understood that the result of the producing instruction is forwarded when the destination register of the producing instruction is the same as either source of the consuming instruction. Thus, we do not explicitly show the bit fields that are compared by the hardware.

▷ Exercise 3.9

This exercise asks, "How much faster would the machine be without any branch hazards?" which should make you immediately think speedup.[1] In this case, we are interested in how the presence or absence of control hazards changes the pipeline speedup. Recall one of the expressions for the speedup from pipelining presented in Chapter 3 of the text:

$$Pipeline\ Speedup = \frac{1}{1 + Pipeline\ Stalls} \times (Pipeline\ Depth) \qquad (3.1)$$

where the only contributions to *Pipeline Stalls* arise from control hazards because the exercise is only focused on such hazards. To solve this exercise, we will compute the speedup due to pipelining both with and without control hazards and then compare these two numbers.

For the "ideal" case where there are no control hazards, and thus stalls, Equation 3.1 yields

$$Pipeline\ Speedup_{ideal} = \frac{1}{1 + 0}\,(4) = 4 \qquad (3.2)$$

where we know from the exercise statement that the pipeline depth is four and the number of stalls is zero because there are no control hazards.

For the "real" case where there are control hazards, the pipeline depth is still four, but the number of stalls is no longer zero as it was in Equation 3.2. To determine the value of *Pipeline Stalls* that includes the effects of control hazards, we need three pieces of information. First, we must establish the "types" of control flow instructions we can encounter in a program. From the exercise statement we know that there are three types of control flow instructions: taken conditional branches, not-taken conditional branches, and jumps and calls. Second, we must evaluate the number of stall cycles caused by each type of control flow instruction. And third, we must find the frequency at which each type of control flow instruction occurs in code. Such values are given in the exercise statement.

To determine the second piece of information, the number of stall cycles created by each of the three types of control flow instructions, we examine how the pipeline behaves under the appropriate conditions. For the purposes of discussion, we will assume the four stages of the pipeline are Instruction Fetch, Instruction Decode, Execute, and Write Back (abbreviated IF, ID,

---

[1] If it does not—shame on you! You call yourself a computer architect?!

Instruction	Clock Cycle					
	1	**2**	**3**	**4**	**5**	**6**
Jump or Call	IF	ID	EX	WB		
$i + 1$		IF	IF	ID	EX	...
$i + 2$			*stall*	IF	ID	...
$i + 3$				*stall*	IF	...

Figure 3.9: Effects of a Jump or Call Instruction on the Pipeline.

EX, and WB, respectively). A specific structure is not necessary to solve the exercise—this structure was chosen simply to ease the following discussion.

First, let us consider how the pipeline handles a jump or call. Figure 3.9 illustrates the behavior of the pipeline during the execution of a jump or call. Because the first pipe stage can always be done independent of whether the control flow instruction goes or not, in cycle 2 the pipeline fetches the instruction following the jump or call (note that this is all we can do—IF must update the PC and the next sequential address is the only address known at this point; however, this behavior will prove to be beneficial for conditional branches as we will see shortly). By the end of cycle 2, the jump or call resolves (recall that the exercise specifies that calls and jumps resolve at the end of the second stage), and the pipeline realizes that the fetch it issued in cycle 2 was to the wrong address (remember, the fetch in cycle 2 retrieves the instruction immediately following the control flow instruction rather than the target instruction) so the pipeline reissues the fetch of instruction $i + 1$ in cycle 3. This causes a one-cycle stall in the pipeline since the fetches of instructions after $i + 1$ occur one cycle later than they ideally could have.

Figure 3.10 illustrates how the pipeline stalls for two cycles when it encounters a taken conditional branch. As was the case for unconditional branches, the fetch issued in cycle 2 fetches the instruction after the branch rather than the instruction at the target of the branch. Therefore, when the branch finally resolves in cycle 3 (recall that the exercise specifies that conditional branches resolve at the end of the third stage), the pipeline realizes it must reissue the fetch for instruction $i + 1$ in cycle 4, which creates the two-cycle penalty.

Figure 3.11 illustrates how the pipeline stalls for a single cycle when it encounters a not-taken conditional branch. For not-taken conditional branches, the fetch of instruction $i + 1$ issued in cycle 2 actually obtains the correct

Instruction	Clock Cycle					
	1	**2**	**3**	**4**	**5**	**6**
Taken Branch	IF	ID	EX	WB		
$i+1$		IF	*stall*	IF	ID	...
$i+2$			*stall*	*stall*	IF	...
$i+3$				*stall*	*stall*	...

Figure 3.10: Effects of a Taken Conditional Branch on the Pipeline.

Instruction	Clock Cycle					
	1	**2**	**3**	**4**	**5**	**6**
Not-Taken Branch	IF	ID	EX	WB		
$i+1$		IF	*stall*	ID	EX	...
$i+2$			*stall*	IF	ID	...
$i+3$				*stall*	IF	...

Figure 3.11: Effects of a Not-Taken Conditional Branch on the Pipeline.

instruction. This occurs because the pipeline fetches the next sequential instruction from the program by default, which happens to be the instruction that follows a not-taken branch. Once the conditional branch resolves in cycle 3, the pipeline determines it does not need to reissue the fetch of instruction $i+1$ and therefore can resume executing the instruction it fetched in cycle 2. Instruction $i+1$ cannot leave the IF stage until *after* the branch resolves because the exercise specifies that the pipeline is only capable of using the IF stage while a branch is being resolved.

Combining all of our information on control flow instruction type, stall cycles, and frequency leads us to Figure 3.12. Note that this figure accounts for the taken/not-taken nature of conditional branches. With this informa-

Control Flow Type	Frequency (per instruction)	Stalls (cycles)
Jumps and Calls	5%	1
Conditional (Taken)	$20\% \times 60\% = 12\%$	2
Conditional (Not-Taken)	$20\% \times 40\% = 8\%$	1

Figure 3.12: A Summary of the Behavior of Control Flow Instructions.

tion we can compute the stall cycles caused by control flow instructions:

$$Pipeline\ Stalls_{real} = (1 \times 5\%) + (2 \times 12\%) + (1 \times 8\%) - 0.37$$

where each term is the product of a frequency and a penalty. We can now plug the appropriate value for *Pipeline Stalls$_{real}$* into Equation 3.1 to arrive at the pipeline speedup in the "real" case:

$$Pipeline\ Speedup_{real} = \frac{1}{1 + 0.37}(4.0) = 2.92 \qquad (3.3)$$

Finding the speedup of the ideal over the real pipelining speedups from Equations 3.2 and 3.3 leads us to the final answer:

$$Pipeline\ Speedup_{without\ control\ hazards} = \frac{4}{2.92} = 1.37$$

Thus, the presence of control hazards in the pipeline loses approximately 37% of the speedup we achieve without such hazards.

▷ Exercise 3.10

These exercises examine a machine with a three-stage pipeline and consider under what conditions adding an additional stage to the pipeline improves performance. The three-stage pipeline consists of these three stages: Instruction Fetch, Operand Decode, and Execution or Memory Access (abbreviated IF, OD, and EM, respectively). The four-stage pipeline is built by adding a Write Back stage (abbreviated WB) to the end of the three-stage pipeline. Before presenting the solution to each exercise, we first develop an equation that is used to solve Exercises 3.10(a) and 3.10(b).

Because time is the final measure of performance, we begin by considering the equation for *CPU Time* from Chapter 1 of the text (as an aside, it is possible to solve these exercises using pipeline speedup; however, such solutions are more involved as you must keep CPI and clock cycle terms consistent):

$$
\begin{aligned}
CPU\ Time &= CPI \times (Clock\ Cycle\ Time) \times (Instruction\ Count) \\
&= CPI \times Clk \times IC \\
&= (CPI_{ideal} + CPI_{stalls}) \times Clk \times IC \qquad (3.4)
\end{aligned}
$$

where CPI_{ideal} is one and CPI_{stalls} represents the CPI due to pipeline stalls. CPI_{stalls} is given by

$$CPI_{stalls} = \sum_{s \in stalls} Penalty_s \times Frequency_s \qquad (3.5)$$

which sums over all types of stalls the product of the frequency of the stall and the stall cost (i.e., the number of penalty cycles the system must remain idle to clear the stall) in cycles.

Using Equation 3.4, we can arrive at a condition that must hold whenever the four stage pipe is a "win" performance-wise:

$$
\begin{aligned}
CPU\ Time_3 &\geq CPU\ Time_4 \\
IC_3 \times (1 + CPI_{stall,3}) \times Clk_3 &\geq IC_4 \times (1 + CPI_{stall,4}) \times Clk_4 \\
(1 + CPI_{stall,3})\,T &\geq (1 + CPI_{stall,4})\,(T - d) \qquad (3.6)
\end{aligned}
$$

where the subscripts on the various terms indicate which pipeline depth the term is associated with and the CPI for stalls is given by Equation 3.5. Because the addition of a stage does not change the number of instructions executed by the machine, the instruction count terms IC_3 and IC_4 are equal and can be canceled. Finally, from the exercise statement, Clk_3 and Clk_4 have been replaced by T and $T - d$, respectively.

In the following exercises, pipeline designs are compared by finding values for the unknowns in Equation 3.6 and then reducing the resulting expression.

▷ Exercise 3.10(a)

This exercise asks us to consider the data hazard outlined in the exercise statement and arrive at a lower bound on the clock cycle reduction, d, which makes moving to a four-stage pipeline profitable in terms of performance. To solve the exercise, we first find values for the CPI due to stalls in both the three-stage and four-stage pipelines, $CPI_{stall,3}$ and $CPI_{stall,4}$, respectively. From the exercise statement, we learn that stalls can potentially occur between instructions i and $i + 1$ and between instructions i and $i + 2$, as summarized in Figure 3.13. A hazard can *not* occur between instruction i and both instructions $i + 1$ and $i + 2$ as the exercise states that "each result has exactly one use." The frequencies are given in the exercise statement, and the penalties can be determined by examining how the pipeline behaves. Because a data hazard can not occur between instructions i and $i + 2$ in the

Data	Frequency	Penalty (cycles)	
Hazard	(per instruction)	3-Stage Pipe	4-Stage Pipe
$i \rightarrow i+1$	$p^{\,1}$	1	2
$i \rightarrow i+2$	p^{-2}	0	1

Figure 3.13: *A Summary of Stall Information for Data Hazards in the Three-and Four-Stage Pipelines.*

three-stage pipeline, the value of the penalty in this case is zero.[2] As an aside, neither pipeline implements split-phase reading/writing of the register file. Such support would require that the three-stage pipeline be able to execute and write a result in the first half of the cycle, which is not likely to be possible for reasonable clock cycles. Because the four-stage pipeline is based upon the three-stage pipeline, we also assume that it also does not implement split-phase reading/writing.

Using the information from Figure 3.13 along with Equation 3.5 developed above for stalls leads to a $CPI_{stall,3}$ of

$$CPI_{stall,3} = 1\left(p^{-1}\right) + 0\left(p^{-2}\right) = \frac{1}{p} \tag{3.7}$$

and a $CPI_{stall,4}$ of

$$CPI_{stall,4} = 2\left(p^{-1}\right) + 1\left(p^{-2}\right) = \frac{2p+1}{p^2} \tag{3.8}$$

Equations 3.7 and 3.8 relate the CPI due to stalls to the parameter p.

To find an expression for the lower bound on the clock cycle reduction, d, required to make moving from a three- to a four-stage pipeline profitable, we can solve for d in Equation 3.6 using the results from Equations 3.7 and 3.8:

$$\left[1 + \left(\frac{1}{p}\right)\right] T \geq \left[1 + \left(\frac{2p+1}{p^2}\right)\right] (T - d)$$

$$d \geq T - \left[T\left(1 + \frac{1}{p}\right)\left(1 + \frac{2p+1}{p^2}\right)^{-1}\right]$$

$$d \geq \frac{T}{p+1} \tag{3.9}$$

---

[2]You should be able to convince yourself this is true by looking at a pipeline diagram.

Equation 3.9 taken as an equality represents the smallest value of d such that the performance, as measured by CPU time, of the four-stage pipeline is at least as good as that of the three-stage pipeline.

▷ Exercise 3.11

In this exercise, we provide the FP data hazard stall detection logic for the DLX pipeline configuration given in Figure 3.44 in the text. The following notes apply to the figures in this solution:

- We provide two figures: Figure 3.14 for the values forwarded to EX/A1 or EX/M1 pipeline stages and Figure 3.15 for the values forwarded to A1/MEM or M1/MEM pipeline stages by store instructions.

- We continue to use the format from earlier exercises. However, when more than one pipeline register is specified in the Source Pipeline Register column, then this implicitly means that the Condition column must check the target register from each of those pipe registers against the sources of the destination instruction (rather than add nearly identical entries for all of the pipe registers). Similarly, when the ALU input could be either top or bottom with no other differences, the entries appear in a single row as well.

- The source registers of the destination instruction are checked in the ID/(EX,M1,A1) pipeline register based on the instruction opcode.

- FP-ALU in Figures 3.14 and 3.15 represents any register-register FP ALU operation.

- We only consider RAW hazards as Exercise 3.14 asks for the WAW information.

- The only instructions that are considered are FP-ALU and FP Store.

Figure 3.14 shows the forwarding logic for data values forwarded to the EX/A1 or EX/M1 stages of the pipeline. Figure 3.15 illustrates data hazards for forwarding to the memory stage if the consuming operation is a store. The figure is almost the same as Figure 3.14; however, since the store instruction does not need the data forwarded until the A1/MEM or M1/MEM stages of the pipeline, it can afford one extra cycle of latency. This has the effect of making load instructions hazard free while decreasing the number of

Source		Destination		Condition
Pipeline Register	Opcode	Opcode	Dest. of Result	
ID/EX	FP Load	FP-ALU	Top/Bot	Destination register of FP Load equals source register of FP-ALU
ID/EX EX/A1 A1/A2 A2/A3	FP Add	FP-ALU	Top/Bot	Destination register of FP Add equals source register of FP-ALU
ID/EX EX/M1 M1/M2 M2/M3 M3/M4 M4/M5 M5/M6	FP Mult.	FP-ALU	Top/Bot	Destination register of FP Mult. equals source register of FP-ALU

Figure 3.14: DLX FP Data Hazard Detection Logic for Forwarding to the EX/M1 or EX/A1 Pipeline Stages.

checks in the pipeline for other instructions. In both Figures 3.14 and 3.15, the phrase "Top/Bot" refers to the top or bottom inputs of the FP-ALU.

▷ Exercise 3.14

In this exercise, we provide the FP WAW data hazard detection logic for the DLX pipeline configuration given in Figure 3.44 in the text. The column headers are slightly different than in Exercise 3.11, but follow the same conventions:

- There are only three ways that a WAW hazard can occur in the DLX FP pipeline: a load after an FP add (which causes 3 stall cycles), a load after an FP multiply (which causes 6 stall cycles), or an FP add after an FP multiply (which causes 3 stall cycles).

- Instructions are checked at IF/ID against other instructions in progress (as in Figure 3.18 in the text).

Source		Destination		Condition
Pipeline Register	Opcode	Opcode	Dest. of Result	
ID/EX EX/A1 A1/A2	FP Add	FP-ALU	Top/Bot	Destination register of FP Add equals source register of FP-ALU
ID/EX EX/M1 M1/M2 M2/M3 M3/M4 M4/M5	FP Mult.	FP-ALU	Top/Bot	Destination register of FP Mult. equals source register of FP-ALU

Figure 3.15: DLX FP Data Hazard Detection Logic for Forwarding to the A1/MEM or M1/MEM Pipeline Stages.

- The "Pipeline Register" indicates the location of the instruction already in the pipe that must write its result before the instruction being checked in IF/ID.

- The operand register specification is unnecessary since we are only concerned with the target register bitfield for comparisons.

Figure 3.16 presents the WAW hazard detection logic for this exercise. In this figure it is understood that the pipeline must be stalled if the destination register of the instruction performing the first write is the same as the destination register of the issuing instruction.

Instruction Performing First Write		Issuing Instruction
Pipeline Register	Opcode	Opcode
ID/A1	FP Add	Load
A1/A2		
A2/A3		
ID/M1	FP Multiply	Load
M1/M2		
M2/M3		
M3/M4		
M4/M5		
M5/M6		
ID/M1	FP Multiply	FP Add
M1/M2		
M2/M3		

Figure 3.16: DLX FP WAW Data Hazard Detection Logic.

Chapter 4

Advanced Pipelining and Instruction-Level Parallelism

Introduction to the Chapter 4 Exercises

Now that Chapter 3 has developed the basics of pipelining, we can look into the interesting stuff. Chapter 4 moves beyond the discussion in Chapter 3 by considering how we might further improve the performance of pipelining. The chapter discusses ways the compiler writer and hardware architect can both influence the effect of hazards and stalls on system performance and the amount of parallelism visible to the system. These hardware and software modifications serve to eliminate some stalls and reduce the CPI in the system. The chapter concludes with an examination of the PowerPC 620, which employs many of the techniques explored in Chapter 4.

▷ Exercise 4.1

There are seven dependences in the C loop presented in the exercise:

1. True dependence from S1 to S2 on a.

2. Loop-carried true dependence from S4 to S1 on b.

3. Loop-carried true dependence from S4 to S3 on b.

4. Loop-carried true dependence from S4 to S4 on b.

5. Loop-carried output dependence from S1 to S3 on a.

6. Loop-carried antidependence from S1 to S3 on a.

7. Loop-carried antidependence from S2 to S3 on a.

For a loop to be parallel, each iteration must be independent of all others, which is not the case in the code used for this exercise.

Because dependences 1, 2, 3, and 4 are "true" dependences, they can not be removed through renaming. In addition, as dependences 2, 3, and 4 are loopcarried, they imply that iterations of the loop are not independent. These factors together imply the loop can not be made parallel as the loop is written. By "rewriting" the loop it may be possible to find a loop that is functionally equivalent to the original loop that can be made parallel. Exercise 4.2 provides an example of such a situation on a different loop.

▷ Exercise 4.4

In this exercise, we are asked to unroll the loop and schedule it for a pipelined version of DLX. We assume that the loop was originally executed a non-zero, even number of times, otherwise, more sophisticated transformations would be required. We have also scheduled the branch-delay slot.

When unrolling a loop with no loop-carried dependences, one can follow some basic guidelines. First, copy all the statements in the original loop and put them after the original loop statements. Second, rename all the registers in the copied instructions so that they are distinct from the original statements (this can be done by adding a fixed value to each register number, assuming there are enough registers available). Third, interleave all of the statements by putting the i'th instruction in the group of copied instructions right after the i'th instruction in the original sequence. These steps yield a schedule without violating data dependences.

One can then remove loop overhead instructions and rearrange other instructions as necessary to cover pipeline latencies. Instructions that use or update index calculations will have to be updated based on reordering of instructions or elimination of intermediate index updates.

Doing these steps and reordering instructions to cover any remaining latencies, yields the code shown in Figure 4.1. In this code, the comments indicate the amount of latency and the instruction from which the latency is measured (e.g., ">1 from LD F0,0(R1)" indicates the instruction must follow the specified load by more than one cycle).

```
loop:   LD      F0,  0(R1)
        LD      F6,  -8(R1)
        MULTD   F0, F0, F2      ; >1 from LD F0
        MULTD   F6, F6, F2      ; >1 from LD F6
        LD      F4,  0(R2)
        LD      F8,  -8(R2)
        ADDD    F0, F0, F4      ; >3 from MULTD F0
        ADDD    F6, F6, F8      ; >3 from MULTD F6
        SUBI    R1, R1, 16
        SUBI    R2, R2, 16
        SD      8(R2), F0       ; >2 from ADDD F0
        BNEZ    R1, loop
        SD      0(R2), F6       ; >2 from ADDD F6,
                                ;  fills branch delay
```

Figure 4.1: Code Unrolled Once and Scheduled.

```
frob:   multd   f0, f2, f4      ; writes f0 on cycle 6
        nop                     ; for timing...
        nop                     ; for timing...
        ld      f6, 0x0667(r16) ; writes f6 on cycle 6
```

Figure 4.2: Code Fragment That Stalls a Tomasulo Machine but Not a Scoreboard Machine.

▷ Exercise 4.8

There are many code sequences that stall a Tomasulo-based system yet do not stall a scoreboard-based system. Such code sequences contain two instructions that have the following features: first, the two instructions attempt to write their results in the same cycle, and second, the two instructions do not utilize the same group of functional units in the scoreboard system.

For example, consider the DLX FP code fragment shown in Figure 4.2. In this code fragment, if we assume the three-stage IS/EX/WR (issue, execute, and write results) Tomasulo pipeline described on page 254 of the text, the pipeline behaves as illustrated in Figure 4.3. In this figure, we have assumed that loads and multiplies spend one and four cycles in execution, respectively. In cycle 6, both the multiply and load instructions attempt to write their results into the register file. It is at this point where things get interesting.

In the scoreboard system the floating-point multipliers and integer unit

Instruction	Clock Cycle					
	1	**2**	**3**	**4**	**5**	**6**
`multd  f0,f2,f4`	IS	EX	EX	EX	EX	WR
`nop`		IS	EX	WR		
`nop`			IS	EX	WR	
`ld     f6,0x0667(r16)`				IS	EX	WR

Figure 4.3: Pipeline Behavior Caused by the Code Fragment.

(which performs the load) have separate result buses (see Figure 4.3 in the text). Therefore, both the multiply and load instructions can write their values into the register file simultaneously.

In the case of Tomasulo's algorithm, the multipliers and load buffers both write their results onto the common data bus, which is the only path into the register file (see Figure 4.8 in the text). As a result, both instructions can not use the common data bus at the same time and one of the instructions must stall a single cycle while the other instruction writes its result into the register file.

▷ Exercise 4.10

To compare the performance of systems with and without a branch target buffer (BTB) for conditional branches we determine the speedup of the CPIs for the two designs, CPI_{BTB} and $CPI_{no\ BTB}$ (we might also approach this exercise by figuring out the speedup of the pipeline with and without the BTB—the resulting speedup equation, when simplified, is identical to the equation for the speedup of the CPIs). The speedup is given by

$$Speedup = \frac{CPI_{no\ BTB}}{CPI_{BTB}} = \frac{CPI_{base} + Stalls_{no\ BTB}}{CPI_{base} + Stalls_{BTB}} \tag{4.1}$$

From the exercise statement we know that CPI_{base} is 1.0, which, by definition, accounts for everything *except* conditional branches. To complete the solution, we must find the number of stall cycles that are caused by unconditional branches in the machines with and without BTBs. To find the stall terms, $Stalls_{BTB}$ and $Stalls_{no\ BTB}$, we begin with the following expression:

$$Stalls = \sum_{s \in Stall} Frequency_s \times Penalty_s \tag{4.2}$$

BTB Result	BTB Prediction	Frequency (per instruction)	Penalty (cycles)
Miss	—	$15\% \times 10\% = 1.5\%$	3
Hit	Correct	$15\% \times 90\% \times 90\% = 12.1\%$	0
Hit	Incorrect	$15\% \times 90\% \times 10\% = 1.3\%$	4

Figure 4.4: A Summary of the Behavior of a BTB for Conditional Branches.

which sums over all stall cases.

The value for $Stalls_{no\ BTB}$ follows simply from the exercise statement and Equation 4.2:

$$Stalls_{no\ BTB} = 15\% \times 2 = 0.30 \tag{4.3}$$

As the system without a BTB has a fixed two-cycle branch penalty, the stall contribution from branches is simply the product of the frequency of branches and the number of penalty cycles. Computing $Stalls_{BTB}$ is a bit more involved.

To find $Stalls_{BTB}$ we must consider each possible BTB outcome from a conditional branch. There are three cases: first, the branch can miss the BTB, second, the branch can hit the BTB and be correctly predicted, and third, the branch can hit the BTB and be incorrectly predicted. Figure 4.4 summarizes these observations. The frequencies and penalties can be found from the exercise statement and the discussion of BTBs in Section 4.3 of the text. For example, if the BTB hits and correctly predicts a branch, there is no penalty (because the BTB returns the next PC in time to be used for the fetch of the instruction following the branch). This case occurs with a frequency per instruction given by the frequency of branches (15%) multiplied by the frequency with which branches are found in the BTB (90%) multiplied by the frequency with which branches in the BTB are predicted correctly (90%).

From Equation 4.2 and Figure 4.4, we can compute $Stalls_{BTB}$:

$$Stalls_{BTB} = (1.5\% \times 3) + (12.1\% \times 0) + (1.3\% \times 4) = 0.097$$

This result along with Equation 4.3 can be plugged into Equation 4.1 to arrive at

$$Speedup = \frac{CPI_{base} + Stalls_{no\ BTB}}{CPI_{base} + Stalls_{BTB}} = \frac{1.0 + 0.30}{1.0 + 0.097} = 1.2$$

Therefore, adding a BTB for conditional branches makes the DLX pipeline about 20% faster.

▷ Exercise 4.14

The answers to these questions can vary widely depending on the assumptions made. We have attempted to outline our assumptions and provide justification, but there are certainly other assumptions that make sense. When assigning these exercises, instructors may wish to closely examine the solutions and perhaps specify some assumptions for you to follow.

These exercises provide an opportunity to compare the performance of several different DLX implementations with a variety of compiler optimizations. The exercises are intended to illustrate that both the architecture and compiler affect system performance. Unfortunately, they are probably the hardest exercises in the text to write solutions to.

There are many different answers to each of the exercises depending on the assumptions you make about the architecture under examination. In an attempt to spell things out, we take a brief detour and discuss some of our assumptions that are common across several parts of this exercise. There are three basic pipeline structures that are considered in this exercise:

1. Classic five-stage DLX with Fetch, Decode, Execute, Memory, Write Back (IF/ID/EX/MEM/WB) pipeline stages used in Exercises 4.14(a), 4.14(b), 4.14(g), 4.14(h), and 4.14(i).

2. DLX implementing Scoreboarding with Issue, Read Operands, Execute, Write Results (IS/RO/EX/WR) pipeline stages used in Exercises 4.14(c) and 4.14(e).

3. DLX implementing Tomasulo's Algorithm with Issue, Execute, Write Results (IS/EX/WR) pipeline stages used in Exercises 4.14(d), 4.14(f), 4.14(j), and 4.14(k).

Each of the sub-exercises explores a variation on one of these general pipeline configurations. As the assumptions outlined in the exercise depend on the type of pipeline under investigation, we briefly address some of the goblins in each of these pipeline configurations that can lunch on the unwary.

The Classic Five-Stage DLX

This pipeline is the easiest to handle as it requires the fewest additional assumptions. For this pipeline, unless otherwise specified, we assume that all of the functional units are fully pipelined as mentioned on page 224 of the text and also are fully bypassed. Next, the latencies in Figures 4.2 or 4.03 of the text can be used as they are specified in these figures (such an assumption is not valid for the other two pipelines). Finally, contention for MEM or WB pipeline stages is resolved by allowing the instruction that issued earliest to complete.

The DLX with Scoreboarding

There are several features of the scoreboarded version of DLX that are open to assumption. Before going into the exercises, we will outline the assumptions we have made for this pipeline structure:

1. An instruction waiting for a result from another functional unit can pass through read operands at the same time the result is being written (see page 245 of the text).

2. An instruction in WR completing will allow a currently active instruction that is waiting on the same functional unit to issue in the same cycle as the first instruction completes WR.

3. Because there is only one integer unit, many integer operations will stall at issue due to the integer unit being busy until WR stage (following the logic in Figure 4.7 in the text).

In addition to these assumptions, we need to know the number of cycles an instruction spends in execution.

For a given instruction, the number of cycles spent in execution is independent of the type of instruction using the result (the number of cycles *between* two instructions to avoid a stall can depend on the types of instructions due to the structure of the pipeline). In Figures 4.2 and 4.63 of the text the latencies are defined as the "distance" between two instructions to avoid a stall. These distances are computed assuming the five-stage pipeline.[1] Thus, the values in these two figures assume a separate MEM stage, something that (according to the text) is not modeled in the scoreboarding machines.

If we examine how many cycles would be needed in the scoreboarding pipeline between the time that an instruction producing a result passes through RO and the time that an instruction that is dependent upon the

---

[1]You should be able to figure out why the latency between two FP operations differs from the latency between an FP operation and a store.

Text Figure	FP Multiply	FP Add
Figure 4.2	3	3
Figure 4.63	6	4

Figure 4.5: Number of Cycles FP Multiplies and Additions Spend in Execution for a Scoreboarding DLX.

result of the first instruction can pass through RO without stalling, it turns out that the amount of time spent in execution is the same as the latencies given in Figures 4.2 and 4.63. Figure 4.5 summarizes the values we use for the number of cycles FP operations spend in the execution stages of the scoreboarding pipeline. As these exercises are only concerned with SAXPY, we only have to worry about FP multiplies and additions. Integer operations only require one cycle in EX as specified in the exercises.

Because most of the exercises using the scoreboard have only one integer unit, performance is poor on SAXPY given the large number of integer operations if you strictly follow the operation of the machine outlined in the text. We have chosen this approach in these solutions even though it makes the scoreboard look comparatively worse. For a more balanced comparison, you may want to consider a scoreboarded DLX with three or four integer units.

The Tomasulo DLX

For the Tomasulo exercises we always assume that any characteristics not explicitly specified in the exercise statement are as shown in Figure 4.8 of the text. In addition, we make the following assumptions:

1. There are enough FP reservation stations to allow an FP operation of any type to be issued each cycle in the absence of stalls. Note that providing lots of reservation stations and fully pipelining a unit are essentially equivalent.

2. There are at least three integer reservation stations so that the machine can issue an integer operation each cycle in the absence of stalls.

3. The EX stage of loads and stores does both the effective address computation and the memory access.

In addition to these assumptions, we need to know the number of cycles an instruction spends in execution.

Text Figure	FP Multiply	FP Add
Figure 4.2	4	4
Figure 4.63	7	5

Figure 4.6: Number of Cycles FP Multiplies and Additions Spend in Execution for a Tomasulo DLX.

As was the case in the scoreboarding exercise, we need to determine values for the number of cycles in execution that are consistent with the latencies described in Figures 4.2 and 4.63 of the text. The motivation, discussion, and procedure are the same with the exception that for the Tomasulo DLX we examine the time between the first EX stage of the producing and consuming instructions as it is at this point that the results are read. It turns out that the amount of time spent in execution is one more than the latencies given in Figures 4.2 and 4.63. Figure 4.6 summarizes the values we use for the number of cycles FP operations spend in the execution stages of the Tomasulo pipeline. As these exercises are only concerned with SAXPY, we only have to worry about FP multiplies and additions. Integer operations only require one cycle in EX as specified in the exercises.

▷ **Exercise 4.14(a)**

Figure 4.7 presents each DLX instruction in the first iteration of the SAXPY loop and identifies the first cycle of execution and number of stall cycles for each instruction using the latencies given in Figure 4.2 of the text. In this exercise we use the standard five-stage IF/ID/EX/MEM/WB pipeline developed in Chapter 3 with fully pipelined FP Multiply and FP Add units. In this figure, cycle 1 is the first cycle the first instruction spends in the EX stage of the pipeline. The number of stall cycles can be found by applying the latencies from Figure 4.2 to the SAXPY code. In each case, the number of stall cycles indicates the number of cycles ID waits before starting EX of the instruction in question.

Ignoring the branch delay in Figure 4.7 that occurs during cycle 15, each iteration of SAXPY takes 14 cycles to complete. Of these 14 cycles, 5 are caused by stalls that can be attributed to the latencies presented in Figure 4.2 of the text. For example, the first multiply must stall one cycle as the proceeding load produces a value that is used as a source by the multiply. As we shall see in the following exercises, we can improve upon this performance through hardware and compiler modifications that reduce both the number

Instruction	First EX Cycle	Stall Cycles	Comments
ld f2,0(r1)	1	0	
	2		multd stalls for f2
multd f4,f2,f0	3	1	
ld f6,0(r2)	4	0	
	5		addd stalls for f4,f6
	6		addd stalls for f4,f6
addd f6,f4,f6	7	2	
	8		sd stalls for f6
	9		sd stalls for f6
sd 0(r2),f6	10	2	
addi r1,r1,#8	11	0	
addi r2,r2,#8	12	0	
sgti r3,r1,done	13	0	
beqz r3,foo	14	0	
	15		beqz delay slot

Figure 4.7: Execution of SAXPY on a Standard Single-Issue DLX.

of stall cycles and improve the number of cycles per iteration.

▷ **Exercise 4.14(d)**

Before building the various tables associated with Tomasulo's algorithm, we need to understand when and where instructions execute. Figure 4.8 presents the execution profile of the first iteration of SAXPY running on a version of DLX that implements Tomasulo's algorithm with the hardware characteristics given in the exercise statement. In this figure, we show the location of each instruction in the machine during execution of the code along with the functional unit and reservation station that processes the instruction. The IS, EX, and WR columns correspond to the issue, execute, and write results stages of the pipeline, respectively. Figure 4.8 can be derived by applying the description of Tomasulo's algorithm presented on page 254 of the text to SAXPY.

Before going any further, make sure you have read through the introduction to Exercise 4.14 on page 62 of this manual, which discusses key

Instruction	Unit & Res. St.	Cycles in			Comments
		IS	EX	WR	
ld f2,0(r1)	Load 1	1	2	3	
multd f4,f2,f0	FP ALU 1	2	3–6	7	
ld f6,0(r2)	Load 2	3	4	5	
addd f6,f4,f6	FP ALU 2	4	8–11	12	Wait for multd
sd 0(r2),f6	Store 1	5	12	—	Wait for addd
addi r1,r1,#8	Integer 1	6	7	8	
addi r2,r2,#8	Integer 2	7	8	9	
sgti r3,r1,done	Integer 3	8	9	10	

Figure 4.8: *Instruction Execution Profile of the First Iteration of SAXPY on a DLX That Implements Tomasulo's Algorithm.*

assumptions.[2] Other noteworthy features of Figure 4.8 include

- The CDB is written to and read from on the same cycle (e.g., examine the relationship between WR and EX for the "ld f2,0(r1)" and "multd f4,f2,f0" instructions).

- Store instructions do not write a result to the CDB.

From Figure 4.8, we determine that the exercise is asking for the state of the machine in cycle 10, when the sgti writes its result on the CDB. We have not included instructions beyond the beqz. By applying the Tomasulo algorithm outlined in the text we can determine the state of the data structures associated with the algorithm.

The first structure we present is the instruction status, which is shown in Figure 4.9 for this exercise. From this figure we can obtain the status of the functional units and reservation stations by noting which instructions have not yet completed. Each instruction that has not yet completed appears in one of the reservation stations of the machine (the specific reservation station depends on how they are allocated during execution—there are many reasonable mappings).

Figure 4.10 presents the reservation station status for this exercise. The fields of each station can be determined by looking at the specific instruction resident in the reservation station. The mapping between active instructions

---

[2]If you are scratching your head after looking at Figure 4.8 it is probably because you have not read the aforementioned discussion!

Instruction	Instruction Status			
	I	**E**	**W**	**Comments**
`ld    f2,0(r1)`	√	√	√	
`multd f4,f2,f0`	√	√	√	
`ld    f6,0(r2)`	√	√	√	
`addd  f6,f4,f6`	√			Executing ...
`sd    0(r2),f6`	√			Waiting for `addd` result
`addi  r1,r1,#8`	√	√	√	
`addi  r2,r2,#8`	√	√	√	
`sgti  r3,r1,done`	√	√		Writing result

Figure 4.9: Instruction Status after the First Iteration of SAXPY on a DLX That Implements Tomasulo's Algorithm.

Function Unit	Reservation Station Status					
	Busy	**Op**	V_j	V_k	Q_j	Q_k
Integer 1	No					
Integer 2	No					
Integer 3	Yes	sgti	r1	done		
FP ALU 1	No					
FP ALU 2	Yes	addd	f4	f6		
FP ALU 3	No					

Figure 4.10: Reservation Station Status after the First Iteration of SAXPY on a DLX That Implements Tomasulo's Algorithm.

and reservation stations can be found in Figure 4.8. To save space we only show the first few reservation stations, as all other stations are not in use.

Finally, Figure 4.11 presents the status of the registers that have yet to be written and any pending stores that have not completed. This figure can be derived by considering which instructions in the reservation stations from Figure 4.10 have yet to write their result along with any stores from Figure 4.9 that have not completed. Any registers not shown in Figure 4.11 are not being written at this point in time.

▷ Exercise 4.14(i)

In this exercise, we are asked to unroll and schedule the SAXPY loop for a VLIW version of DLX defined in Figure 4.29 in the text (this version is

Field	Register Status		
	r3	f6	Store 1
Q_i	Integer 3	FP ALU 2	FP ALU 2

Figure 4.11: Register Result and Store Buffer Status after the First Iteration of SAXPY on a DLX That Implements Tomasulo's Algorithm.

derived from the standard five-stage DLX). The latencies for the instructions are given in Figure 4.2 in the text. As in Exercise 4.14(h), we assume that the number of iterations will be a multiple of four. To unroll the loop, the body was copied four times, and the loop overhead instructions removed (the extra loop index checks, loop index increments, and branch instructions).

The processor can issue one integer, two memory operations, and two floating-point instructions every cycle under the restriction that there are no dependences between instructions issued in the same cycle. We assume that a VLIW instruction cannot issue until all the operands for all the instructions are available.

Figure 4.12 shows how the instructions have been packed into VLIW instructions and the cycle number at which each VLIW instruction begins execution. All instructions that issue at the same time were packed into the same instruction word. The Pipeline column of the figure shows which pipeline a specific instruction was statically scheduled in. If we don't count branch delay slots, each iteration executes in 13 cycles. Given that there are 24 instructions in the loop, the sustained rate is only about 2 instructions per clock out of a possible 5.

▷ Exercise 4.14(k)

Exercise 4.14(k) should reference Figure 4.34 in the text, not Figure 4.31.

Before building the various tables associated with a speculative processor, we need to understand when and where instructions execute. Figure 4.13 presents the execution profile of the first two iterations of SAXPY running on a three-issue speculative version of DLX. In this figure, we show the location of each instruction in the machine during execution of the code along with the functional unit and reservation station (load and store reservation stations are actually entries in the reorder buffer) that process the instruction. The IS, EX, and WR columns correspond to the issue, execute, and write results

Issue Cycle	Instruction		Pipeline
1	LD	F2, 0(R1)	Memory 1
	LD	F8, 8(R1)	Memory 2
2	LD	F14, 16(R1)	Memory 1
	LD	F20, 24(R1)	Memory 2
3	LD	F6, 0(R2)	Memory 1
	LD	F12, 8(R2)	Memory 2
4	LD	F18, 16(R2)	Memory 1
	LD	F24, 24(R2)	Memory 2
	ADDI	R1, R1, #32	Integer
5	MULTD	F4, F2, F0	FP ALU 1
	MULTD	F10, F8, F0	FP ALU 2
	ADDI	R2, R2, #32	Integer
6	MULTD	F16, F14, F0	FP ALU 1
	MULTD	F22, F20, F0	FP ALU 2
	SGTI	R3, R1, done	Integer
9	ADDD	F6, F4, F6	FP ALU 1
	ADDD	F12, F10, F12	FP ALU 2
10	ADDD	F18, F16, F18	FP ALU 1
	ADDD	F24, F22, F24	FP ALU 2
12	SD	-32(R2), F6	Memory 1
	SD	-24(R2), F12	Memory 2
13	SD	-16(R2), F18	Memory 1
	SD	-08(R2), F24	Memory 2
	BEQZ	R3, foo	Integer

Figure 4.12: Execution Schedule for VLIW Version of SAXPY.

Instruction	Unit & Res. St.	Cycles in			Comments
		IS	EX	WR	
`ld    f2,0(r1)`	Load 1	1	2	3	
`multd f4,f2,f0`	FP ALU 1	1	3–9	10	Wait for `ld`
`ld    f6,0(r2)`	Load 2	2	3	4	
`addd  f6,f4,f6`	FP ALU 2	2	10–14	15	Wait for `multd`
`sd    0(r2),f6`	Store 1	3	15	—	Wait for `addd`
`addi  r1,r1,#8`	Integer 1	3	4	5	
`addi  r2,r2,#8`	Integer 2	4	5	6	
`sgti  r3,r1,done`	Integer 3	5	6	7	
`beqz  r3,foo`	Integer 1	6	7	8	
`ld    f2,0(r1)`	Load 1	7	8	9	
`multd f4,f2,f0`	FP ALU 3	7	11–17	18	
`ld    f6,0(r2)`	Load 2	8	9	10	
`addd  f6,f4,f6`	FP ALU 4	8	18–22	23	Wait for `multd`
`sd    0(r2),f6`	Store 2	9	10	—	
`addi  r1,r1,#8`	Integer 1	9	10	11	
`addi  r2,r2,#8`	Integer 2	10	11	12	
`sgti  r3,r1,done`	Integer 3	11	12	13	
`beqz  r3,foo`	Integer 1	12	13	14	

Figure 4.13: Instruction Execution Profile of the First Two Iterations of SAXPY on a DLX That Implements Tomasulo's Algorithm Extended for Multiple-Issue and Speculative Execution.

stages of the pipeline, respectively. Figure 4.13 can be derived by applying the description of Tomasulo's algorithm presented on pages 310–312 of the text (extended to allow multiple issues per cycle) to SAXPY.

Before going any further, make sure you have read through the introduction to Exercise 4.14 on page 62 of this manual (this discusses some key assumptions). Other noteworthy features of Figure 4.13 include

- The bookkeeping required to commit results mentioned on page 312 of the text is assumed to be taken care of during the WR pipeline stage.

- In-order issue is assumed. That is, an instruction can not issue until all preceding instructions have issued.

- The CDB has been widened to accommodate up to three completions per cycle (to balance the ability to issue up to three instructions per cycle). This modification is hinted at in the caption of Figure 4.34 in the text.

- The CDB can be written to and read from on the same cycle (e.g., examine the relationship between WR and EX for the "ld f2,0(r1)" and "multd f4,f2,f0" instructions).

- Store instructions do not write a result to the CDB.

From Figure 4.13, we determine that the exercise is asking for the state of the machine in cycle 12, when the beqz issues for the second time. By applying the speculative Tomasulo algorithm outlined in the text we can determine the state of the data structures associated with the algorithm.

The first structure we present is the reorder buffer (ROB) status, which is shown in Figure 4.14 for this exercise. Rather than assume any particular size, we show the ROB entries for all of the instructions that have been issued at the time we examine the ROB. The entries in the ROB appear in the order in which they issue in the program. The individual fields can be found by applying the speculative algorithm from the text.

To arrive at this figure, we place instructions into the ROB in the order in which they issue in Figure 4.13. Next, the state is filled in with the last pipeline stage completed by cycle 12. To decide which instructions have committed, we walk through the ROB entries in ascending order until we find an entry that has not completed writing its result. Entries before this entry can be marked as committed. Marking entries as completed in this fashion ensures that instructions commit their state to the machine's "permanent" state in program order. At this point in the code, ROB entry 4 is the next to commit at cycle 15 after it writes its result.

The value and destination fields are filled in based on the instruction. In these two columns "#i" refers to ROB entry i, "$M[j]$" refers to the contents of memory location j, and "$R[k]$" refers to the value of register k in the register file. When an instruction requires the value of register i, it gets it from the "latest" busy entry in the ROB that specifies register i as a destination, or if there is no such entry in the ROB, from the register file. For example, consider ROB entry 11. In this case, the instruction needs the value of f0 and f2. The value for f0 is taken from the register file as there is no busy ROB entry that specifies f0 as a destination. On the other hand, the value for f2 is taken from ROB entry 10, which is the last busy entry to specify f2 as a destination. This technique ensures that data dependences within the code are honored.

Ent.	Reorder Buffer Status				
	Busy	**Instruction**	**State**	**Dest.**	**Value**
1	No	ld f2,0(r1)	CM	f2	$M[0 + R[\text{r1}]]$
2	No	multd f4,f2,f0	CM	f4	$\#1 \times R[\text{f0}]$
3	No	ld f6,0(r2)	CM	f6	$M[0 + R[\text{r2}]]$
4	Yes	addd f6,f4,f6	EX	f6	$\#2 + \#3$
5	Yes	sd 0(r2),f6	IS	$0 + R[\text{r2}]$	$\#3$
6	Yes	addi r1,r1,#8	WR	r1	$R[\text{r1}] + 8$
7	Yes	addi r2,r2,#8	WR	r2	$R[\text{r2}] + 8$
8	Yes	sgti r3,r1,done	WR	r3	$\#6 > \text{done}?$
9	Yes	beqz r3,foo	WR		
10	Yes	ld f2,0(r1)	WR	f2	$M[0 + \#6]$
11	Yes	multd f4,f2,f0	EX	f4	$\#10 \times R[\text{f0}]$
12	Yes	ld f6,0(r2)	WR	f6	$M[0 + \#7]$
13	Yes	addd f6,f4,f6	IS	f6	$\#11 + \#12$
14	Yes	sd 0(r2),f6	IS	$0 + \#7$	$\#13$
15	Yes	addi r1,r1,#8	WR	r1	$\#6 + 8$
16	Yes	addi r2,r2,#8	WR	r2	$\#7 + 8$
17	Yes	sgti r3,r1,done	EX	r3	$\#15 > \text{done}?$
18	Yes	beqz r3,foo	IS		

Figure 4.14: Reorder Buffer Status after the First Two Iterations of SAXPY on a DLX That Implements Tomasulo's Algorithm Extended for Multiple-Issue and Speculative Execution.

Function Unit	Reservation Station Status						
	Busy	Op	V_j	V_k	Q_j	Q_k	Dest.
Integer 1	Yes	beqz			#17		
Integer 2	No						
Integer 3	Yes	sgti	#15	done			#17
FP ALU 1	No						
FP ALU 2	Yes	addd	#2	#3			#4
FP ALU 3	Yes	multd	#10	$R[\text{f0}]$			#11
FP ALU 4	Yes	addd	#11			#12	#13

Figure 4.15: Reservation Station Status after the First Two Iterations of SAXPY on a DLX That Implements Tomasulo's Algorithm Extended for Multiple-Issue and Speculative Execution.

Given the execution profile and ROB status, we can obtain the contents of the reservation stations (RS) by noting which instructions have not yet completed writing their results (the specific reservation station depends on how they are allocated during execution—there are many reasonable mappings). Once an instruction writes its results, the RS is released, and the ROB is used to hold the result. Also, keep in mind that the ROB entry functions as the RS for load and store instructions. Figure 4.15 illustrates the status of the RS for this exercise. The mapping between active instructions and reservation stations can be found in Figure 4.13. To save space we only show the first few reservation stations, as all other stations are not in use. The various fields can be determined by looking at the sources and destination of the instruction in conjunction with the ROB status presented in Figure 4.14. The Q_j and Q_k fields are only used while the instruction is waiting for the j or k operand to be computed. Once a value is known, it is moved into the V_j or V_k entry in the RS.

Figure 4.16 presents the status of the registers in the machine. Any registers not shown in this figure are not being written by any instructions currently active in the ROB. The entries in Figure 4.16 show which registers are being written by active instructions and the ROB entry that produces the *next* value of the register. For example, active (i.e., busy) ROB entries 4, 12, and 13 all produce a value of f6, but as instructions commit in order, the next value of f6 is given by ROB entry 4. When ROB entry 4 retires, the register status of f6 is updated to indicate that ROB entry 12 is the next ROB entry to produce a value of f6.

Field	FP & Integer Register Status					
	r1	r2	r3	f2	f4	f6
ROB Entry	#0	#7	#8	#10	#11	#4
Busy	Yes	Yes	Yes	Yes	Yes	Yes

Figure 4.16: Register Result Status after the First Two Iterations of SAXPY on a DLX That Implements Tomasulo's Algorithm Extended for Multiple-Issue and Speculative Execution.

Finally,[3] from Figure 4.13 we can see that each iteration of SAXPY requires 15 cycles to execute. This value is determined by considering the cycle by which all instructions in the first iteration have written their results. Over half of this time is spent waiting for the multiply and add to complete because the first iteration is done issuing at cycle 6! If you recall the solution to Exercise 4.14(j), you should note that the multiple issue has allowed the "front end" of the machine to get farther into the code but has not improved the time to execute an iteration.

▷ Exercise 4.17

For a true dependence to potentially exist, the indices used to access the array must be the same, so for some values of i and j, $ai + b$ is equal to $cj + d$. This formulation accounts for the case where there are loop-carried dependences also. Thus,

$$\begin{aligned} ai + b &= cj + d \\ ai - cj &= d - b \end{aligned} \tag{4.4}$$

The values of a and c can be expressed as follows:

$$a = g \prod_x a_x \tag{4.5}$$

$$c = g \prod_y c_y \tag{4.6}$$

where g is the greatest common divisor of a and c and the a_x and c_y terms are the remaining integral factors.

---

[3] I thought Exercise 4.14 would never end!

Plugging Equations 4.5 and 4.6 into Equation 4.4 yields

$$\left(g\prod_x a_x\right)i - \left(g\prod_y c_y\right)j = d - b$$

and thus

$$\left(\prod_x a_x\right)i - \left(\prod_y c_y\right)j = \frac{d-b}{g} \tag{4.7}$$

The left-hand side of Equation 4.7 must be an integer because all of the left-hand side terms are integral. Thus, $\frac{d-b}{g}$ must also be an integer. By definition, g is simply $\mathrm{GCD}(a,c)$ and therefore for a true dependence to exist, $\mathrm{GCD}(a,c)$ must divide $d-b$ evenly.

Keep in mind that the GCD test is a necessary, but not sufficient condition for the existence of a dependence. Although it may indicate a dependence between $ai+b$ and $cj+d$, the range over which i and j iterate also comes into play. For example, the GCD test may indicate dependence even though $ai+b$ is always between 0 and 100 and $cj+d$ is always between 1000 and 1100.

▷ Exercise 4.18

To rewrite the software pipelining example on page 294 in the text, we need to examine what the loop currently does. Since the branch test at the bottom of the loop exits after the last element of the array is loaded, we need to make sure that that actually happens. As written in the text, an element two past the end of the array is loaded during the final iteration. Instead, what we want is for element M[n] (assuming M has n elements) to be stored during the first iteration.

If we change the offsets so that the SD instruction stores at 16(R1) instead of 0(R1) and the LD instruction accesses 0(R1) instead of -16(R1), then to make the loop run properly, the SD instruction must be storing M[n]. Since we now store at 16(R1), we need to decrement R1 by 16 prior to the loop so that M[n] is the element stored during the first iteration of the new loop. Making these changes yields the code in Figure 4.17 (the startup and cleanup code will be explained below). Now that we know how the loop body will look, we can decide what needs to be done in the startup and cleanup code by examing what happens during the first and last iterations of the new loop.

```
        LD      F0, 0(R1)        ; Load   M[n]
        ADDD    F4, F0, F2       ; Add to M[n]
        SD      0(R1), F4        ; Stores M[n]

        SUBI    R1, R1, 16       ; Set loop counter

        ; M[n] is first element stored in the loop
        ; M[3] is last element stored in the loop

loop:
        SD      16(R1), F4       ; Stores M[i]
        ADDD    F4, F0, F2       ; Add to M[i-1]
        LD      F0, 0(R1)        ; Load   M[i-2]
        SUBI    R1, R1, #8
        BNEZ    R1, Loop

out_of_loop:
        ST      16(R1), F4       ; Stores M[2]
        ADDD    F4, F0, F2       ; Add to M[1]
        ST      8(R1), F4        ; Stores M[1]
```

Figure 4.17: Reengineered Software Pipelined Loop.

During the last iteration of the loop, the old value of M[1] is loaded, the new value of M[2] is computed, and the new M[3] is stored. Thus, when the loop is over, the new value of M[2] needs to be stored and the new value of M[1] needs to be computed and stored. Similarly, during the first iteration of the new loop, the new value of M[n] is stored, the new value of M[n-1] is computed, and the old value of M[n-2] is loaded. These changes are reflected in the cleanup and startup code in Figure 4.17.

▷ Exercise 4.20

Both the reorder buffer and reservation stations can provide the values of source operands in a speculative processor. This design seems to be inefficient as values end up being duplicated. This exercise explores the reasons behind this decision and shows how a speculative DLX would have to change if the value field in the reservation stations were removed.

```
addd    f0,f4,f4      ; ROB[0] = f0
multd   f1,f4         ; ROB[1] = f1
                      ; ROB[0] retires here
subd    f2,f0,f1      ; ROB[2] = f2
divd    f3,f4,f4      ; reuses ROB[0]
```

Figure 4.18: Code Sequence That Does Not Work Properly if Reservation Stations Do Not Have Value Fields.

▷ **Exercise 4.20(a)**

The primary reason value fields must be present in both the reservation stations (RS) and the reorder buffer (ROB) is that ROB entries have finite lifetimes. Consider what happens when instruction i in an RS uses the value held in ROB entry j as one of its source operands. As long as instruction i begins execution before ROB entry j is committed to the register file, the RS need not have a value field because the RS can retrieve the operand value from the ROB. On the other hand, if ROB entry j is committed to the register file before instruction i begins execution, instruction i can not determine the value held in RS j, as committing the ROB entry releases the entry back into the pool of free ROB entries. In this case, it is possible for a source value used by instruction i to become corrupted.

Figure 4.18 provides an example of a piece of code that does not work on a machine without value fields in the RS. For the purposes of this discussion we assume that the machine has a three-entry ROB, FP adds take one cycle while FP multiplies take ten cycles to execute, and the machine has enough functional units to issue all instructions in the sequence without stalling. The code begins by allocating ROB entries 0 and 1 for the add and multiply instructions. The subtract is dispatched to the RS but must wait for its operands to become available. Before the multiply can complete and the divide can dispatch the add retires and releases ROB entry 0 after updating the register file. Thus, when the divide dispatches it uses ROB entry 0. Once the multiply completes, the subtract can execute, but it no longer can obtain the correct value of f0 from ROB entry 0 as the divide has overwritten it!

To generate code that would work if the RS does not have value fields, we simply find a code sequence that either always finds its operands in the register file or that does not have the potential for an instruction using a "stale" ROB entry as shown above. Such code is shown in Figure 4.19. In this code, we assume that instruction latencies are such that the source

```
addd    f0,f4,f4        ; f4 is in register file
subd    f1,f4,f4
subd    f2,f4,f4
addd    f2,f0,f0        ; f0 is in register file
```

Figure 4.19: Code Sequence That Does Work Properly if Reservation Stations Do Not Have Value Fields.

operands are always in the register file by the time an instruction dispatches. This assumption implies that code without this property, such as that shown in Figure 4.18, may or may not work correctly on the machine!

For the machine structure outlined in Section 4.6 of the text, reservation stations must have a value field for each possible source operand of a given operation to avoid using corrupted data, unless the program can be guaranteed to behave in a particular fashion. Relying on the ROB to hold the values and eliminating value fields from the RS requires changing the behavior of the machine (see Exercise 4.20(b) for more information) to ensure correct operation in the general case.

Chapter 5

Memory-Hierarchy Design

Introduction to the Chapter 5 Exercises

Chapter 5 begins to move outside the domain of the CPU by considering the top levels of the memory hierarchy. The chapter begins with an introduction of the principle of locality from which the development of caches naturally follows. After exploring caches and how their performance can be improved, the text discusses the operation and performance of main memory and virtual memory. With the development of the memory hierarchy complete, issues such as speculative execution or cache coherency can be considered in greater depth to illustrate how the memory hierarchy influences the design of other portions of the system. Finally, the chapter considers the memory hierarchy of the Alpha AXP 21064 to illustrate many of the points considered in the chapter.

▷ Exercise 5.1

This exercise uses differences in cache organizations to illustrate how benchmarks can present a skewed perspective of system performance. Because system performance is heavily influenced by the memory hierarchy (if you do not believe this, take a look at Figure 5.1 in the text again!), it is possible to develop code that runs poorly on a particular cache organization. This exercise should drive home an appreciation for not only the influence of cache organization on performance, but also an appreciation of how difficult it is for a single program to provide a reasonable summary of *general* system performance.

```
foo:    beqz    r0, bar         ; branch iff r0 == 0
        .
        .
        .
bar:    beqz    r0, foo         ; branch iff r0 == 0
```

Figure 5.1: DLX Code That Performs Better on Cache A.

▷ Exercise 5.1(a)

In this exercise we develop a program that causes Cache A to perform much better than Cache B. Consider the DLX code blurb shown in Figure 5.1. We make two assumptions in this code: first, the value of r0 is zero; second, locations foo and bar both map onto the same set in both caches. For example, foo and bar could be 0x00000000 and 0x80000000 (these addresses are in hexadecimal, by the way), respectively, since both addresses reside in set zero of either cache.

On Cache A, this code only causes two compulsory misses to load the two instructions into the cache. After that point, all accesses generated by the code hit the cache. For Cache B, all the accesses miss the cache. This occurs because a direct-mapped cache can only store one block in each set, yet the program has two active blocks that map to the same set. The cache will "thrash" because when it generates an access to foo, the block containing bar is resident in the cache, and when it generates an access to bar, the block containing foo is resident in the cache.

This is a good example of a case where a victim cache (discussed in the text and in the paper "Improving Direct-Mapped Cache Performance by the Addition of Small Fully-Associative Cache and Prefetch Buffers" by Jouppi[1]) could eliminate the performance benefit of the associative cache. Keep in mind that in this example the information on which Cache B misses is always recently resident.

▷ Exercise 5.1(c)

In computing the speedup between these two cache designs, we ignore compulsory misses and the time required to execute the instructions. Our analysis concentrates on the time to perform the memory accesses. The code

---

[1] This paper appeared in the *Proceedings of the 17th Annual International Symposium on Computer Architecture*, May 1990, pp. 364–373.

in Exercise 5.1(a) requires one read access to read each of the two `beqz` instructions from the program. When this code is run on Cache A, each instruction access hits the cache (remember, we ignore compulsory misses). Thus, the total time required to process cache accesses for the code presented in Figure 5.1 of Exercise 5.1(a) on Cache A is nh_a where n is the number of instructions executed and h_a is the hit time on Cache A. On Cache B the code from Figure 5.1 causes a miss on each instruction access. For n instructions, the total time to process all cache accesses is $10h_b n$ where n is the number of instructions executed and $10h_b$ is the miss time on Cache B (recall that the exercise states that misses take ten times as long as hits on both caches). The *miss time* can be contrasted with the *miss penalty*, another parameter used in Chapter 5 of the text to describe the amount of time required to process a miss. While the miss time represents the total time required to process a miss, the miss penalty represents the time above and beyond the hit time required to process a miss. If we assume that $h_a = h_b$, then Cache A will run the code from Exercise 5.1(a) ten times faster than Cache B (this falls out of the speedup between the two caches given by $\frac{10h_b n}{h_a n}$).

The hit time is a critical cache parameter, and our assumption that $h_a = h_b$ may not always hold in the RealWorld as a direct-mapped cache can have a smaller hit time than an associative cache. Mark Hill (the author of the DineroIII cache simulator) uses differences in hit times in "A Case for Direct-Mapped Caches"[2] to show that even though direct-mapped caches have larger miss rates than associative caches, the smaller hit time of a direct-mapped cache allows them to provide similar performance levels.

▷ Exercise 5.3

> *Make sure you understand the program from Exercise 5.2 that generates the graph for this exercise.*

This question asks the reader to determine various attributes of the cache on a SPARCstation 1+ given a graph of the runtimes of the program from Exercise 5.2 (Figure 5.54 in the text). This program records the amount of time required to step through arrays of several different sizes at various strides. From these read and write times it is possible to infer various details of the SPARCstation's cache such as its total size. The graph used in this

---

[2]This article appeared in *IEEE Computer*, 21(12):25–40, December 1988.

exercise plots the time to read and write to the array computed by the program for multiple array sizes and strides (strides are measured in bytes on this graph). Each individual line on the graph corresponds to a different array size (the legend at the bottom of the plot shows the data point markers used for each total array size) while the stride is indicated along the x axis. The total time to read and write to the array is shown along the vertical axis.

▷ Exercise 5.3(a)

Because the time to read and write the array goes up dramatically for array sizes larger than 64K, we conclude that the smaller arrays fit in cache, and so the cache must be 64K bytes. The rise in read and write time occurs because of the miss penalty. If the accesses all fit in cache, the amount of time spent processing misses is zero. However, once accesses start missing the cache, the time spent processing misses rises, causing the total time to rapidly rise (recall that memory access times are typically much larger than cache access times).

▷ Exercise 5.4

The two parts of this exercise illustrate how, in general, write through caches require much more bandwidth to the memory system than write back caches. This should have some intuitive appeal as a write through cache generates a write to main memory every time the cache is written to while a write back cache can only write to main memory when a block is replaced.

▷ Exercise 5.4(a)

To determine the amount of bandwidth currently in use, we must determine how many accesses are presented to the memory system on average. Because the system contains a cache, each access generated by the processor may or may not result in an access to memory, as the access may be serviced by the cache and not require help from the memory system. We begin the solution by examining what a cache can do when it receives an access from the processor. If the access hits the cache, the following pertains:

- On a read hit the cache contains the data in question and therefore does not need to generate a memory system access.

Access Hits Cache?	Access Type	Frequency	Mem. Accesses Generated
Yes	Read	$95\% \times 75\% = 71.3\%$	0
Yes	Write	$95\% \times 25\% = 23.8\%$	1
No	Read	$5\% \times 75\% = 3.8\%$	2
No	Write	$5\% \times 25\% = 1.3\%$	3

Figure 5.2: Summary of Memory Accesses Generated by a Write Through Cache.

- On a write hit a write through cache updates both the value in the cache and the value in main memory. Thus, the cache must generate a memory access to update the word in memory being written to cache.

If the access misses the cache, the following is true:

- On a read miss the cache fills the appropriate cache block from memory, which requires two memory system reads as each block is two words.

- On a write miss the cache first fills the appropriate cache block from memory requiring two memory system reads. Next, the cache writes the word of data to main memory as the cache is write through.

Summarizing the behaviors described above along with specific information from the exercise statement leads to Figure 5.2, which provides an overview of how processor accesses map onto memory system accesses in the presence of a write through cache. The frequency column is given by the product of the hit or miss frequency with the read or write frequency. As a cache block is two words and the memory system can read one word at a time, cache block fills require two accesses.

The average number of accesses to the memory system from the cache can be computed by summing the product of the frequency and the number of accesses from Figure 5.2 across all possible situations. Doing so yields

$$
\begin{aligned}
Accesses_{avg} &= (71.3\% \times 0) + (23.8\% \times 1) + (3.8\% \times 2) + (1.3\% \times 3) \\
&= 0.35
\end{aligned}
$$

Thus, every access to cache results in an average of 0.35 accesses to main memory. We can determine the bandwidth used in this system by computing the number of accesses generated by the system and dividing this result by the number of accesses the memory system can support:

$$Bandwidth\ Used = \frac{0.35\,(10^9)}{10^9} = 35.0\%$$

The numerator is the product of the average number of accesses to the memory system generated by each cache access and the number of accesses the processor makes to the cache. The denominator is the total bandwidth the memory system can support. The result indicates that 35% of the available bandwidth to the memory system is used to support the cache in this scenario.

▷ Exercise 5.5

The two parts of this exercise ask us to evaluate the performance of a write back and write through cache design. To perform this evaluation, we turn yet again to our old friend and standard of performance: time. You should be familiar with the following equation for CPU time developed in Section 5.2 to account for the memory hierarchy:

$$CPU\ Time = IC \times \left(CPI_{execution} + \frac{Memory\ Stall\ Cycles}{Instruction} \right) \times Clk \quad (5.1)$$

To estimate the performance of the two cache designs, we assume the instruction counts and clock cycles are the same in the write through and write back cache systems. This assumption allows us to focus on the CPI term in the middle of Equation 5.1. In the following discussion, we outline a general approach that can be used to solve the parts of this exercise.

We begin by examining the CPI due to execution, $CPI_{execution}$, which accounts for the cycles taken to *execute* an instruction in the *absence* of memory stalls. If we know the number of cycles and frequency of each type of instruction executed by the system we can compute this CPI from

$$CPI_{execution} = f_{loads}\,CPI_{loads} + f_{stores}\,CPI_{stores} + f_{other}\,CPI_{other} \quad (5.2)$$

The instruction set is partitioned into the these three groups (loads, stores, and other) because from the standpoint of the cache, there are only three types of instructions in the system. That is, all of the instructions in one of these three groups look the same to the cache in that the cache behaves in the same manner for any instruction within a group. The frequencies and CPIs in Equation 5.2 can be determined from Figure 2.26 in the text and the exercise statements, respectively. The execution CPI does not take into account two sources of stalls:

- Those caused by fetching instructions from memory.

- Those caused by load or store instructions when they access data.

Rest assured, these oversights are only temporary; they are accounted for in the memory stalls per instruction term of Equation 5.1.

To determine the appropriate number of memory stalls per instruction, we break the stall term into two parts: one to represent stalls on instruction fetch and another to represent stalls on data accesses by loads and stores. Thus, the memory stall term in Equation 5.1 becomes

$$\frac{Memory\ Stall\ Cycles}{Instruction} = \frac{I\ Fetch\ Stall\ Cycles}{Instruction} + \frac{Data\ Stall\ Cycles}{Instruction} \quad (5.3)$$

where the fetch and data stall terms are of the form given in Section 5.2:

$$\frac{Stall\ Cycles}{Instruction} = \frac{Memory\ Accesses}{Instruction} \times Miss\ Rate \times Miss\ Penalty$$

For fetch stalls, the number of memory accesses per instruction is one as all instructions require one memory access to fetch each instruction. In the case of data stalls, only load and store instructions have a data memory access that implies that the number of memory accesses per instruction for data accesses is $f_{loads} + f_{stores}$ (essentially, we are evaluating this expression: *Average Accesses* $= \sum Frequency \times Accesses$). Substituting this information into Equation 5.3 yields

$$\frac{Memory\ Stall\ Cycles}{Instruction} = (R_i P_i) + [(f_{stores} + f_{loads})\, R_d P_d] \quad (5.4)$$

where R is a miss rate, P is a miss penalty, and f is a frequency. The subscripts indicate the specific miss rate, miss penalty, or frequency (e.g., i implies instruction fetches, d implies data accesses, etc.). With Equations 5.1, 5.2, and 5.4 we can examine the relative performance of the two caches under a variety of circumstances.

▷ Exercise 5.5(a)

Solving this exercise is a matter of plugging values into Equations 5.2, 5.4, and 5.1. We begin by examining the execution CPI. The exercise states that cache reads or writes require one or two cycles in the absence of memory-related stalls on either cache organization, respectively. Therefore, load and store instructions have CPIs of one and two, respectively. Also, we assume that "other" instructions execute in a single cycle in the absence of memory stalls (which is reasonable for a pipelined system). Therefore, the execution CPI for either cache organization is given by

$$CPI_{execution} = (f_{loads} \times 1) + (f_{stores} \times 2) + (f_{other} \times 1) \qquad (5.5)$$

where the values for f_{loads}, f_{stores}, and f_{other} can be determined from Figure 2.26 of the text.

For memory stalls from instruction fetches, the miss rate, R_i in Equation 5.4, is that of the instruction cache, which is given as 0.5% in the exercise statement. The miss penalty, P_i in Equation 5.4, accounts for the time required to fill a cache block from main memory and is given as 50 cycles in the exercise statement. We assume that the instruction cache is not written to (i.e., no self-modifying code) and therefore does not contain dirty blocks, which implies that there is never write back traffic.

For stalls from data accesses, the miss rate, R_d in Equation 5.4, is the miss rate of the data cache, which is given as 1.0% in the exercise statement. The miss penalty, P_d in Equation 5.4, depends on cache organization, unlike the penalty for instruction fetch stalls. On write misses both write through and write back caches must fill a cache block from main memory, which requires 50 cycles according to the exercise statement (the time to service a cache miss). Additionally, in a write back cache a miss implies that a block is being flushed from cache. If this block is dirty (which happens 50% of the time), the contents of main memory must be updated before the block is filled, requiring an *additional* 50-cycle penalty to write the dirty block. Therefore, P_d for a write back cache is 75 (from $50 + (50\% \times 50)$) and is 50 for a write through cache.

Substituting the values from the above discussion into Equation 5.4 leads to two expressions for the average number of memory stall cycles per instruction. For a write through cache

$$\frac{Memory\ Stall\ Cycles}{Instruction} = (1.0\% \times 50) + (f_{stores} + f_{loads})(1.0\% \times 50) \quad (5.6)$$

and for a write back cache

$$\frac{Memory\ Stall\ Cycles}{Instruction} = (1.0\% \times 50) + (f_{stores} + f_{loads})(1.0\% \times 75) \quad (5.7)$$

Program	Execution CPI	Write Through		Write Back	
		Stalls	Total CPI	Stalls	Total CPI
compress	1.05	0.38	1.43	0.44	1.49
eqntott	1.00	0.41	1.41	0.48	1.48
espresso	1.04	0.38	1.42	0.45	1.49
gcc	1.14	0.44	1.58	0.53	1.67
li	1.16	0.49	1.65	0.61	1.77
Average	1.08	0.42	1.50	0.50	1.58

Figure 5.3: Cache Performance for Several SPECint92 Programs.

where f_{loads} and f_{stores} are taken from Figure 2.26 of the text.

Using Equations 5.5, 5.6, and 5.7 allows us to determine the total CPI term of the CPU time equation. Figure 5.3 summarizes the results for both the write back and write through caches. In this figure, the CPI terms in the write through and write back columns are the sum of the execution CPI and the memory stall cycles given in the stalls column. The average values are the arithmetic means over all of the programs. Because the instruction count and clock cycle terms of the CPU time are the same in this scenario, we only present the CPI terms in Figure 5.3.

As measured by CPU time, the write back cache is roughly 5% slower than the write through cache using the average numbers. The difference is attributable to the need to occasionally write back data to main memory. In this scenario, this write back cache must see the latency associated with the write back while the write through never sees its equivalent latency (because write throughs use a write buffer that never stalls the cache). The improved performance does not come without a price, unfortunately. Because write through caches always send writes to main memory, they tend to eat up more of the bandwidth to main memory (see Exercise 5.4 for an interesting example). One final point to consider is how write back caches impact memory-mapped I/O locations or shared data in a multiprocessor system. Remember that in a write back cache individual writes to a cache block are not seen by main memory unless the block is flushed from cache after every write!

▷ Exercise 5.6

The example cited by this exercise begins on page 403 of the text

```
/* loop with last 7 iterations split to avoid
 * extraneous prefetches
 */
for ( j=0; j<93; j++ ) {
    prefetch( b[j+7][0] );    /* prefetchs elements 7-99 */
    prefetch( a[0][j+7] );    /* prefetchs elements 7-99 */
    prefetch( a[1][j] );      /* prefetchs elements 0-92 */
    a[0][j] = b[j][0] * b[j+1][0];
}

/* last iterations with prefetches */
for ( j=93; j<100; j++ ) {
    prefetch( a[1][j] );      /* prefetchs elements 93-99 */
    a[0][j] = b[j][0] * b[j+1][0];
}
```

Figure 5.4: Alterations to First Loop Nest to Avoid Unnecessary Prefetches.

rather than page 401 as stated in the exercise.

In this exercise, we are asked to fix up the example starting on page 403. There are two things that can be done to improve execution time: eliminate extraneous prefetches and reduce the number of non-prefetched cache misses. For the remainder of this solution, our remarks on the example refer to the code at the top of page 404 (the solution to the example). Also, from the discussion in the text, one can gather that the cost to execute a prefetch instruction is one cycle.

Eliminating extraneous prefetches can be done easily by splitting loops so that the final iterations of the loop that do not need to prefetch are separate from those iterations that do need to prefetch. Eliminating all cache misses is not possible. Also, without completely rewriting the code, some misses to a in the first loop are unavoidable.

Thus, our approach will be as follows: split loops where necessary to eliminate extraneous prefetch instructions and add prefetches during the first loop nest to avoid the misses to a in the second loop nest.

We start with the first loop nest and split it so the last iterations are in a loop that do no prefetching for the current iterations at all. We also add prefetches for the elements of a[1][ ]. When the code shown in Figure 5.4 finishes execution, all of b and all of a[0][ ] and a[1][ ] will be in cache.

Moving on to the second loop nest from the original code, since all of a[1][ ] is in cache (due to earlier prefetches), we only need to prefetch a[2][ ] during the i=1 loop. We also split off the i=2 loop so we can write it with no prefetches (since that is the last loop iteration and there is nothing to prefetch). Since we have now split the entire i loop into separate code segments, there is no need to have any i-loop at all. Making these changes results in the code shown in Figure 5.5. Figuring out the cost of all this is easy:

- Each iteration of the first new loop nest costs 10 cycles per iteration and there are 93 iterations.

- Each iteration of the second new loop nest costs 8 cycles per iteration and there are 7 iterations.

- Each iteration of the third new loop nest costs 8 cycles per iteration and there are 100 iterations.

- Each iteration of the fourth new loop nest costs 7 cycles per iteration and there are 100 iterations.

There are still 11 cache misses in the first loop nest, which will add 550 clocks to the execution time. However, there are no cache misses in any of the remaining loops, so we can just add up all the numbers:

$$
\begin{aligned}
Time &= (10 \times 93) + (8 \times 7) + (8 \times 100) + (7 \times 100) + 550 \\
&= 3036
\end{aligned}
$$

Thus, our result is 3036 cycles for the new and improved code compared to the 3450 cycles for the example in the text.

▷ Exercise 5.8

This exercise evaluates the performance of a system with a cache and TLB. The first two parts of the exercise explore the CPI of the system with real caches and TLBs while the third part discusses some performance issues related to TLBs and caches. In this manual, we only present the solution for the first part of the exercise. Our solution is based on the following expression for CPI:

$$
CPI = CPI_{execution} + \frac{Memory\ Stall\ Cycles}{Instruction} \tag{5.8}
$$

```
/* This is the code that would have been executed in
 * the i=1 loop
 */
for ( j=0; j<100; j++ ) {
    prefetch( a[2][j] );   /* prefetch all elements for */
                           /*    next loop nest         */
    a[1][j] = b[j][0] * b[j+1][0];
}

/* This is the code that would have been executed in
 * the i=2 loop
 */
for ( j=0; j<100; j++ ) {
    a[2][j] = b[j][0] * b[j+1][0];
}
```

Figure 5.5: Altered Second Loop Nest That Avoids Unnecessary Prefetches and Cache Misses.

This equation is the CPI term of the CPU time equation developed in Section 5.2 of the text to account for the memory hierarchy. In the following discussion, we outline a general approach that can be used to solve the first two parts of this exercise (even though only the solution to Exercise 5.8(a) is presented in this manual).

We begin by examining the CPI due to execution, $CPI_{execution}$, which accounts for the cycles taken to *execute* an instruction in the *absence* of memory stalls. For this exercise, we make the reasonable assumption that all instructions execute in one cycle in the absence of memory stalls. By definition, the execution CPI does not take into account three sources of stalls:

- Those caused by fetching instructions from memory.

- Those caused by load or store instructions when they access data.

- Those caused by the TLB.

These stalls are accounted for in the memory stalls per instruction term of Equation 5.8.

To determine the appropriate number of memory stalls per instruction, we break the stall term into three parts based on the sources of stalls listed above:

$$\frac{Memory\ Stalls}{Instruction} = \frac{I\ Fetch\ Stalls}{Instruction} + \frac{Data\ Stalls}{Instruction} + \frac{TLB\ Stalls}{Instruction} \quad (5.9)$$

where the fetch and data stall terms are of the form given in Section 5.2:

$$\frac{Stall\ Cycles}{Instruction} = \frac{Memory\ Accesses}{Instruction} \times Miss\ Rate \times Miss\ Penalty$$

The exact form of the TLB term Equation 5.9 is not required to solve Exercise 5.8(a) as this term is zero for the ideal TLB used in Exercise 5.8(a).

For fetch stalls, the number of memory accesses per instruction is one, as all instructions require one memory access to fetch each instruction. In the case of data stalls, only data access instructions have a data memory access, which implies that the number of memory accesses per instruction for data accesses is simply the frequency of data access instructions. Substituting this information into Equation 5.3 yields

$$\frac{Memory\ Stall\ Cycles}{Instruction} = (R_i P_i) + (f_{data} R_d P_d) + 0 \quad (5.10)$$

where R is a miss rate, P is a miss penalty, and f_{data} is the frequency of data access instructions. The subscripts indicate the specific miss rate, miss penalty, or frequency (e.g., i implies instruction fetches, d implies data accesses, etc.). With Equations 5.8 and 5.10 we can evaluate the performance of the caches for Exercise 5.8(a).

▷ Exercise 5.8(a)

The CPI for the three cache organizations assuming the TLB is ideal can be found using Equations 5.8 and 5.10. In the expression for memory stalls, Equation 5.10, the term for TLB stalls is zero as the TLB in this exercise is ideal and therefore can not stall the CPU. Also, all three cache configurations are unified, which implies that the miss rate and penalties are independent of the type of access (i.e., data versus instruction). In terms of Equation 5.10 this observation implies that $R_i = R_d$ and $P_i = P_d$. Substituting this information along with the frequency of data accesses (20% from the exercise statement) and the execution CPI (assumed to be one as per the discussion above) into Equations 5.8 and 5.10 leads to

$$\begin{aligned} CPI &= 1.5 + [RP + (RP \times 20\%) + 0] \\ &= 1.5 + 1.2RP \end{aligned} \quad (5.11)$$

| Configuration | Cache | | CPI |
	Miss Rate	Miss Penalty	
16KB Direct	0.029	72	4.0
16KB Two-Way	0.022	72	3.4
32KB Direct	0.020	72	3.2

Figure 5.6: Summary of the Performance of Several Caches with an Ideal TLB.

where R is the miss rate and P is the miss penalty for the unified cache.

The miss rate, R, depends on the specific cache under consideration and can be found from the results presented in Figure 5.9 of the text. For a write back cache, the miss penalty depends on the time required to flush and fill a cache block. Block flushes and fills both require 48 clocks to complete, according to the exercise statement (40 clocks for memory latency and 8 clocks to fill the 32-byte block at 4 bytes per clock). While a block fill must always occur on a miss, a block flush only occurs if the block being replaced is dirty, which happens 50% of the time, according to the exercise. Thus, the miss penalty is 72 cycles (from the expression $48 + (50\% \times 48) = 72$). Keep in mind that the caches do not have a write buffer and thus the miss penalty needs to account for the time required to do the flush.

Plugging these values into Equation 5.11 leads to the results shown in Figure 5.6. These numbers should help you appreciate how much the memory hierarchy can impact performance. Even with miss rates down around 2%, the memory hierarchy accounts for around 60% of the total CPI because of the huge penalty for missing the cache.

▷ Exercise 5.10

The exercise involves applying number theory to the problem of computing modulo arithmetic for the purpose of building memory systems that have a prime number of memory banks. The foundation of the approach is the realization that numbers modulo $2^N - 1$ can sometimes be computed more easily than computing remainders (referred to as *mod* for the rest of this question) for arbitrary number pairs.

The idea involves decreasing the number of address bits that need to be examined by the hardware to compute the result. By reducing the number of bits sufficiently, the value of the *mod* operation can be looked up in a small ROM.

Looking at Insight 3 in the exercise introduction in the text, as long as $2^N - 1$ is a prime number, we can compute the value of $\left(a \bmod \left(2^N - 1\right)\right)$ using a generalization of the formula presented. For the special case of $2^N - 1 = 7$, we get

$$a \bmod 7 = 1 \times (a_0 + a_3 + ...) + 2 \times (a_1 + a_4 + ...) + 4 \times (a_2 + a_5 + ...) \quad (5.12)$$

Thus, by examination, we see that the value computed on the right-hand side of Equation 5.12 can fit in many fewer than the original 32 bits required to store a. In fact, that number of bits required to represent the value is so small, the new value can be used as an input to a ROM that stores 3-bit quantities at each location, each of which represents the original value *mod* $2^N - 1$.

▷ Exercise 5.10(a)

In Exercise 5.10(a), we are asked to derive the general formula for deciding how many bits are needed as input to a ROM in order to look up the result of a mod operation.

Assume that we have an M bit address and $2^N - 1$ banks and $2^N - 1$ is a prime number. When the address is translated using the approach in Insight 3 in the text, there will be N terms (numbered from 0 to $N - 1$) where the i'th term will be

$$2^i \times \sum_{j=0}^{\left\lceil \frac{M}{N} \right\rceil - 1} a_{i+N \times j} \quad (5.13)$$

For simplicity, we will always use the value of $\left\lceil \frac{M}{N} \right\rceil$ to represent the number of terms in each summation even though this slightly overestimates the number of bits needed. Since each term is the sum of $\left\lceil \frac{M}{N} \right\rceil$ bits, the maximum value of each term is

$$Term_i = 2^i \times \left\lceil \frac{M}{N} \right\rceil$$

Adding all the terms yields

$$Max\ Value = \sum_{i=0}^{N-1} Term_i$$

and the total number of bits required to represent a number of this size is

$$Bits = \lceil log_2 \left(Max\ Value \right) \rceil$$

If we plug in the values $M = 32$, $N = 3$, the result is

$$Bits_{M=32,N=3} = 7$$

▷ Exercise 5.14

The two parts of this exercise (of which only the first is solved in this manual) explore how cache performance can be counter-intuitive. One would expect a fully associative cache to outperform a direct-mapped cache because associativity is "good," right? Not quite—cache behavior is a strange and wondrous thing ...

▷ Exercise 5.14(a)

A small direct-mapped cache can potentially outperform a fully associative cache if the system is executing a loop that does not fit entirely in cache. To see how this can happen, consider a loop that accesses three unique addresses: A, B, and C and then repeats the sequence by looping back to A. The reference stream for such a program would look like this: **ABCABCABC** ... , where each letter corresponds to an address in the reference stream. To simplify the discussion, we assume that our caches have only two blocks of storage space with addresses A and C mapping into the first block and address B mapping into the second block. For a fully associative version of the two-block cache, our reference stream always misses the cache if the replacement policy is LRU. Such behavior does not occur in a direct-mapped cache using LRU replacement because each address maps into a specific location of the cache. In the direct-mapped version, we only miss on an access to A or C but we always hit on an access to B (ignoring initial compulsory misses).

Essentially, what happens is that the direct-mapped cache allows only certain addresses to be placed into a given block. This allows blocks to be "protected" in the sense that they can not be replaced by just any access, but rather only by accesses whose addresses also map into the same block. In our two-block caches let us consider the state of the direct-mapped cache right before address C is accessed. Figure 5.7 shows how the direct-mapped

Reference	Cache Contents before Reference		Action
	Block 1	**Block 2**	
C	A	B	Miss, Replace A
A	C	B	Miss, Replace C
B	A	B	Hit
C	A	C	Miss, Replace A

Figure 5.7: Operation of a Two-Block Direct-Mapped Cache.

Reference	Cache Contents before Reference			Action
	Block 1	**Block 2**	**LRU**	
C	A	B	A	Miss, Replace A
A	C	B	B	Miss, Replace B
B	C	A	C	Miss, Replace C
C	B	A	A	Miss, Replace A

Figure 5.8: Operation of a Two-Block Fully Associative Cache.

cache behaves during an iteration of the reference stream. In steady state, the reference stream generates one hit and two misses. In the case of the fully associative cache, the behavior is as shown in Figure 5.8. For the fully associative cache, all references always miss as the reference stream is just a bit too big to fit fully in cache.

Chapter 6

Storage Systems

Introduction to the Chapter 6 Exercises

Chapter 6 continues to move the discussion of the text outside the domain of the CPU by moving further down the memory hierarchy. This chapter of the text focuses on storage systems and their performance. The presentation opens by discussing the types of storage systems and how they can be connected to a system. Next, the discussion moves to performance measurement of storage systems and techniques to improve their reliability and availability along with some of the issues that impact both storage systems and other parts of the complete system. The chapter concludes with an exploration of the performance of the UNIX file system.

About the Fallacy on Page 549 and Figures 6.43 and 6.2

The second equation presented in this fallacy (attributed to Chen and Lee) provides a more accurate model of the seek time of a disk as a function of the distance of the seek. In this equation there are three parameters, a, b, and c, which according to the text:

> are selected for a particular disk so that this formula will match the quoted times for Distance = 1, Distance = max, and Distance = 1/3 max.

Several of the exercises require the use of the seek time equations from this fallacy along with the equations for a, b, and c given in Figure 6.43 in the text. In most cases, the exercises ask the reader to use the disk parameters

99

outlined in Figure 6.2. Under these circumstances, the values of a, b, and c do not hold the relationships stated in the text.

Namely, if we use the expressions for a, b, and c presented in Figure 6.43 along with the disk parameters from Figure 6.2 we find an expression for the seek time based on the form specified by Chen and Lee. However, if we take this equation and substitute Distance = 1/3 max, we do not find the seek time is the average seek time which the text states should be the case.

In several of the coming solutions we were unable to arrive at reasonable values for a final answer due to this limitation. Rather than derive our own values for a, b, and c, we have elected to simply point out how one would proceed and provide a solution technique rather than an exact solution.

▷ Exercise 6.3

The statistics in Figure 6.44 present the percentages of all seeks that fall within a particular distance. To find the average seek distance of the two workloads, we simply take a weighted average of the seek distance. In this case, the weights are the frequence of a range of seeks. For example, in the case of the UNIX workload:

$$
\begin{aligned}
Dist_{avg} = \ & (0 \times 24\%) + (8 \times 23\%) + (24 \times 8\%) + (38 \times 4\%) + \\
& (54 \times 3\%) + (68 \times 3\%) + (84 \times 1\%) + (98 \times 3\%) + \\
& (114 \times 3\%) + (128 \times 2\%) + (144 \times 3\%) + (158 \times 2\%) + \\
& (174 \times 3\%) + (188 \times 3\%) + (300 \times 15\%) \\
= \ & 75.14
\end{aligned} \tag{6.1}
$$

A similar computation for the business workload leads to an average seek distance of 12.49. Note that both of these are much smaller than the average distance specified by the "one-third" rule of thumb.

▷ Exercise 6.5

There are a few typos in the first printing of the second edition of the text. In Exercise 6.5(c), the question should read "1000 MB/sec," not "100 MB/sec." Also, the TP-1 benchmark mentioned in the question refers to the DebitCredit benchmark described in the text.

This exercise explores the performance and cost of a system that uses the TP-1 benchmark as its workload.

▷ Exercise 6.5(c)

In this question, we are asked how fast the CPU would have to be before it could flood the bus with requests. Since the current bus can handle 2,621,440 TP/s and the current CPU can handle 8000 TP/s, the CPU would have to be

$$\frac{2,621,440}{8,000} = 328$$

times faster than the current CPU. Since the current CPU is 800 MIPS, the new CPU would have to be 262,400 MIPS.

▷ Exercise 6.6

The statement for this exercise leaves out the required seek time parameters of the disk needed to solve for an exact solution. The solution presented here is a general approach.

In this question, we are asked to compute the number of 4KB I/Os per second and the MB/sec achieved for two different disk configurations. Since the megabytes can be computed from the number of I/Os by multiplying by the I/O size, we will concentrate on computing the number of I/Os per second. We start by using the formula for average disk access time given in the book:

$$Access\ Time_{avg} = Time_{seek} + Time_{rot\ lat} + Time_{xfer} + Time_{cont} \quad (6.2)$$

where $Time_{seek}$, $Time_{rot\ lat}$, $Time_{xfer}$, and $Time_{cont}$ are the times for seek, rotational latency, transfer, and the controller, respectively.

For the controller time, we assume that it only needs to be paid for the first sector of a particular sequential read and its cost is given as

$$Time_{cont} = 2\text{ms}$$

The average rotational latency can be computed based on the assumption that, on average, the disk has to rotate half way around to find the right sector. Since the disk is rotating at 7200 RPM, we get

$$Time_{rot\ lat} = \frac{1}{2} \times \frac{1}{7,200} = 4.2\text{ms}$$

To compute the transfer time, note that 7200 RPM is equivalent to 120 RPS and

$$120 \text{ RPS} \times 16 \text{ sectors} = 1920 \text{ sectors/sec}$$

So, each sector spends $\frac{1}{1920}$ or $520\mu s$ under the disk head. Since each sector has 1KB, this means that the maximum transfer rate is 1.9MB/sec per disk (so the four-disk disk array has a transfer rate of 7.6MB/sec). The formula for transfer time for a message of size N is

$$Time_{xfer} = \frac{N}{1.9\text{MB}}$$

Since the question asks for 4KB reads and we are told that the sectors are stored sequentially, we will assume for the single-disk case that the rotational latency only has to be paid for the first 1KB and that the other three sector reads only cost the time required by the transfer rate. With these assumptions, the transfer time for the single-disk configuration is

$$Time_{xfer} = \frac{4,096}{1,900,000} = 2.1\text{ms}$$

and the cost for the four-disk configuration is one-fourth that or 0.53ms.

The only thing left is the seek time. We are told to use the formulas from the Fallacy section, but the specific parameters of the disk (minimum seek time, maximum seek time, and average seek time) are unspecified in the question. Thus, we will answer this question without using specific values for a, b, and c, knowing that they could be computed if the disk seek specifications were provided.

To compute the seek time, we are told the requests are random, so that the average distance in tracks is 1/3 of 885, or 295 tracks. We assume that the sectors are on the same surface for each 4KB read and that the time to switch surfaces can be overlapped with the seek time. The formula for seek time is

$$Seek\ Time = a \times \sqrt{294} + b \times (294) + c$$

Now the average access time for either disk configuration can be computed by plugging the terms into Equation 6.2 above.

If we take the inverse of the average access time, we get the number of I/Os per second that a disk configuration can handle:

$$I/Os\ per\ second = \frac{1}{Access\ Time}$$

Then, to compute the MB/s of I/O, we just multiply by the size of each I/O:

$$MB/sec = 4\text{KB} \times I/Os\ per\ second$$

▷ Exercise 6.10

These exercises explore the effect of the write policy of a system's cache on the ability of a system to perform I/O. Most of the time the CPU will find information it needs in its caches and thus not have to use the system bus to access main memory.[1] As a result, during the times the CPU does not need to access main memory (i.e., during cache hits), the bus is free to be used by I/O devices to handle DMA accesses.

In this exercise, you first determine how much of the time the bus is available given a write back or write through cache and then use these results to determine how many disk accesses could occur in the free time. Chapter 5 is a good resource to brush up on cache behavior should that be necessary.

▷ Exercise 6.10(a)

For this solution, we assume you have a complete understanding of the mechanics of caches. If you need to brush up on cache behavior check out Chapter 5 in the text. Also, the solution to Exercise 5.4 might be helpful in understanding this solution. In this exercise we assume that there are two devices using the system bus: the cache and a DMA I/O controller. Exercise 6.10(a) asks us to find the percentage of all cycles during which the bus is busy servicing requests from the cache.

An expression that proves useful when attempting to evaluate such percentages is the CPI of the system. Recall a form of the CPI expression developed in Chapter 5 that accounts for the memory hierarchy:

$$
\begin{aligned}
CPI &= CPI_{ideal} + \frac{Memory\ Stall\ Cycles}{Instruction} \\
&= CPI_{ideal} + \left[\left(\frac{Memory\ References}{Instruction} \right) \times \left(\frac{Memory\ Stall\ Cycles}{Memory\ Reference} \right) \right]
\end{aligned}
$$

---

[1] At least, this is how things should be in theory...

Instruction Class	Frequency	Cycles	Read Accesses	Write Accesses
Loads	22.8%	2	2	0
Stores	14.3%	2	1	1
Other	62.9%	1	1	0

Figure 6.1: Instruction Mix Characteristics.

This equation provides us with the answer to the exercise, provided we make one assumption. Because the exercise states that DMA I/O can occur simultaneously with cache hits, we assume that this implies that DMA I/O is prevented from using the bus during the times when the cache requires the bus (for write throughs, write backs, or cache block fills). Such an assumption implies that the cache is only "on" the bus when it is involved in a memory stall cycle. In other words,

$$Traffic\ Ratio = \frac{Memory\ Stall\ Cycles\ per\ Instruction}{CPI_{ideal} + Memory\ Stall\ Cycles\ per\ Instruction} \quad (6.3)$$

This ratio works out to be in "units" of stalls per cycle, which is what we are after, assuming that the bus is busy whenever the CPU stalls due to the memory system. We can now solve for each of the terms in this equation.

Before going further, it is helpful to summarize the characteristics of the instruction mix we are using to evaluate the system. This information is collected from the exercise statement along with the **gcc** column of Figure 2.26 in the text and presented in Figure 6.1.

The number of accesses in this figure includes both instruction and data accesses, as should be obvious from our understanding of load/store instruction sets such as DLX.[2] With the numbers in this figure we can compute all manner of interesting parameters:

- Memory Accesses per Instruction: 1.37

- Memory Reads per Instruction: 1.23, 90% of all memory accesses

- Memory Writes per Instruction: 0.14, 10% of all memory accesses

- CPI with a perfect memory system: 1.37

---

[2]If not, back to Chapter 2 with you!

Access Hits Cache?	Access Type	Frequency	Cycles Bus Is Busy
Yes	Read	$95\% \times 90\% = 85.5\%$	0
Yes	Write	$95\% \times 10\% = 9.5\%$	16
No	Read	$5\% \times 90\% = 4.5\%$	23
No	Write	$5\% \times 10\% = 0.5\%$	39

Figure 6.2: Summary of Bus Behavior Caused by Each Access to a Write Through Cache.

Each of these parameters is independent of the cache write policy and can be computed from the information in Figure 6.1 using equations similar to the CPI equation from Chapter 1. The only information that remains unknown in Equation 6.3 is the number of memory stall cycles per memory reference, which can be determined by considering the cache organization.

Figure 6.2 summarizes the number of stall cycles per memory access for the write through cache.[3] In this figure, the number of cycles the bus is busy is the same as the average number of cycles the CPU stalls for the cache to service each request. For the write through cache, there are four possible results from an access, based on whether or not the access hits and whether it is a read or a write. The frequencies in Figure 6.2 are computed by taking the product of the hit or miss frequency with the read or write frequency.

Figure 6.3 summarizes the number of stall cycles per memory access for the write back cache. As was the case for the write through summary, the number of cycles the bus is busy is the same as the average number of cycles the CPU stalls for the cache to service each request. For the write back cache, there are four possible results from an access, based on whether or not the access hits and whether the block being replaced is dirty. The frequencies in Figure 6.3 are computed by taking the product of the hit or miss frequency with the clean or dirty block frequency.

With the information in Figures 6.2 and 6.3 we can determine the average number of stall cycles per access by summing the product of the frequency and the penalty for each case. Doing so for the write through cache using the information from Figure 6.2 results in the following:

$$\begin{aligned} \textit{Stalls per Access} \quad = \quad & (85.5\% \times 0) + (9.5\% \times 16) + \\ & (4.5\% \times 23) + (0.5\% \times 39) \end{aligned}$$

---

[3]We assume a write-allocate policy for the write through cache because the exercise states that the whole block is read on *any* miss.

Access Hits Cache?	Is Block Dirty?	Frequency	Cycles Bus Is Busy
Yes	No	95% × 70% = 66.5%	0
Yes	Yes	95% × 30% = 28.5%	0
No	No	5% × 70% = 3.5%	23
No	Yes	5% × 30% = 1.5%	31

Figure 6.3: Summary of Bus Behavior Cause by Each Access to a Write Back Cache.

$$= 2.75$$

Using the information from Figure 6.3 for the write back cache yields

$$
\begin{aligned}
\textit{Stalls per Access} \ = \ & (66.5\% \times 0) + (28.5\% \times 0) + \\
& (3.5\% \times 23) + (1.5\% \times 31) \\
= \ & 1.27
\end{aligned}
$$

Thus, every access to cache generates an average of 2.75 or 1.27 stall cycles for the write through or write back caches, respectively.

Finally, to compute the traffic ratio, we simply substitute the appropriate values into Equation 6.3, which, for the write through cache is:

$$\textit{Traffic Ratio}_{thru} = \frac{1.37\,(2.75)}{1.37 + [(1.37)\,(2.75)]} = 73.3\%$$

and for the write back cache is:

$$\textit{Traffic Ratio}_{back} = \frac{1.37\,(1.27)}{1.37 + [(1.37)\,(1.27)]} = 56.0\%$$

These results should agree with our intuition that write back caches generally require less bus bandwidth to support as they only write to main memory on block flushes.

▷ Exercise 6.10(b)

This exercise requires the ability to subtract. We are interested in finding the amount of "excess" bus bandwidth given that the bus can be loaded to 80% of its capacity without slowing the system. From Exercise 6.10(a), the write through and write back caches require 73.3% and 56.0% of the bus bandwidth, respectively. Thus, with a write through cache, 6.7% of the bandwidth is available, while in a write back cache 24.0% is available.

▷ Exercise 6.17

If the value of C is changed to 2 we can no longer use the simplified form of the time spent in the queue, $Time_{queue}$, used in the example. Instead, we must use the following general form:

$$Time_{queue} = Time_{server} \frac{(1 + C) \times (Server\ Utilization)}{2\,(1 - Server\ Utilization)}$$

which reduces to the form used in the example when C is 1.

From the example, the server utilization is independent of the variance and thus remains 0.2. However, the value of t_{queue} changes:

$$Time_{queue} = (20\text{ms}) \frac{(1 + 2) \times (0.2)}{2\,(1 - 0.2)} = 7.5\text{ms}$$

Thus, increasing the variance increases the time spent in the queue, which should have some intuitive appeal given that the variance represents the "spread" of values around the mean. From Figure 6.23, the 90th percentile is 2.8 times the mean for a C of 2, which implies that the 90th percentile of the queuing time is $2.8 \times 7.5\text{ms} = 21.0\text{ms}$. Finally, the time spent in the system is simply the sum of t_{queue} and $Time_{server}$ or $7.5\text{ms} + 20\text{ms} = 27.5\text{ms}$. Again, what we see in this example is an increase in the average time spent in the system caused by an increase in the variance of the time.

▷ Exercise 6.19

Consulting the discussion of automated tape libraries on page 494 in Section 6.2 of the text, the automatic tape library the exercise refers to holds a total of 60 terabytes.[4]

As there are 10 tape readers in the system, to read the entire library of 6000 tapes each tape reader must read 600 tapes. To read the library efficiently we assume that we are assigning 600 unique tapes to each of the 10 readers. The time required to switch between these 600 tapes is $600 \times 30\text{s} = 1.8 \times 10^4\text{s}$ which is the product of the number of tapes and the time to switch tapes. Note that this represents the time to walk through the *entire* tape library as the tape changing can occur in parallel (that is, each of the 10 readers reads its first tape, then each switches to its second tape, and so on).

---

[4] For this solution, we use 10^{12} bytes.

The time required to actually read the information on all 6000 tapes can be found by dividing the total capacity of the library (60 terabytes) by the total bandwidth of the tape readers (10 readers at $9MBs^{-1}$ per reader, or $90MBs^{-1}$ total). Again, we assume the 10 tape readers operate in parallel. This implies that it takes 6.7×10^5s to read the data.

The total time is given by the sum of the time to load tapes (1.8×10^4s) and the time to read tapes (6.7×10^5s). Thus, it takes roughly 6.9×10^5s, or 7.92 days, to read the entire 6000-tape library!

Chapter 7

Interconnection Networks

Introduction to the Chapter 7 Exercises

In Chapter 7, the text explores interconnection networks. The discussion begins by developing terminology to describe the operation and performance of networking schemes by examining a simple two-computer network. The chapter then briefly discusses how the network can be connected to a computer and the types of media that are typically used to implement the network itself. With the basics of interconnection networks discussed, the chapter explores how we might go about connecting more than two computers together by exploring several popular interconnection topologies. Chapter 7 concludes with a presentation of some of the cross-cutting issues along with a brief discussion of ATM.

To remain consistent with the text and industry, we will use powers of ten when computing network bandwidths in this chapter. In other words, a megabit per second is 10^6 bits per second rather than 2^{20} bits per second.

▷ Exercise 7.1

Figure 7.1 shows the delivered bandwidth for payload data in megabits per second at message sizes of 32, 300, 600, 900, 1200, and 1500 bytes. For each message size, the bandwidth was computed assuming that 90% of the 10 Mbits/sec is available bandwidth and that there is a startup time of 500 microseconds regardless of message size.

For each Ethernet packet, there is 26 bytes of overhead for headers, checksums, and padding. Since the minimum packet size that Ethernet will

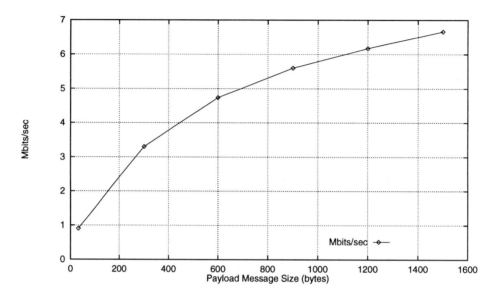

Figure 7.1: Delivered Bandwidth versus Message Size.

send is 64 bytes, the 32-byte message will have to include an additional 6 bytes of padding. None of the other message sizes will require padding to reach the 64-byte minimum. The size of a message in bytes (except for messages with 32-byte payloads) is

$$Message\ Size = Payload\ Size\ in\ Bytes + 26$$

The time to send the message in seconds is

$$Send\ Time = 5.0 \times 10^{-4} + \frac{Message\ Size \times 8}{90\% \times (10 \times 10^6)}$$

and the delivered bandwidth in millions of bits per second is

$$Bandwidth = \frac{Message\ Size \times 8}{Send\ Time \times 10^6}$$

▷ Exercise 7.3

This exercise compares SneakerNet (or at least an overnight version) with the net to show how network performance compares with other forms of information "transportation." To solve this exercise, we simply apply the equation for transfer time developed in the text:

$$Transfer\ Time = \frac{Amount\ of\ Data}{Transfer\ Rate} \qquad (7.1)$$

By turning this equation around we can find an expression for the rate of transfer in terms of the time and the amount of data.

▷ **Exercise 7.3(a)**

We begin the solution by considering the overnight delivery service. Moving the 100GB of data across the United States takes 15 hours using the overnight delivery service. In this case, the transfer time is independent of the amount of data being transferred, unlike the relationship shown in Equation 7.1.

For the network links, we can apply Equation 7.1, assuming that the information is effectively transmitted at one-half the speed of the slowest link, as all information must pass through this link and only one-half its bandwidth may be utilized. On the route where the T1 line is the slowest link, the transfer time is

$$Transfer\ Time = \frac{100 \times 10^9 \times 8\text{b}}{50\% \times \left(1.5 \times 10^6 \text{bs}^{-1}\right)} = 1.1 \times 10^6 \text{s}$$

or roughly 318 hours. For the Ethernet-limited route, the transfer time is

$$Transfer\ Time = \frac{100 \times 10^9 \times 8\text{b}}{50\% \times \left(10 \times 10^6 \text{bs}^{-1}\right)} = 1.7 \times 10^5 \text{s}$$

or roughly 48 hours. In both of these results, the 50% accounts for the fact that you can only use one-half of the bandwidth at the slowest link, and the size of the tape is converted from bytes into bits. Given these results, the overnight delivery beats either network route handily.

▷ **Exercise 7.5**

This exercise asks us to provide several switch setups to achieve various design goals (minimum hardware cost, minimum latency, and balanced bandwidth).

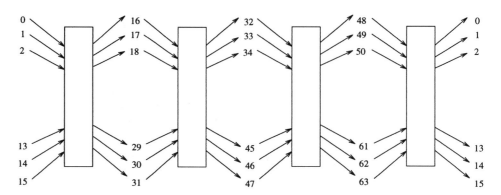

Figure 7.2: Minimum Number of Switches to Connect 64 Hosts.

The only part available is a 16 × 16 ATM switch, which we assume to be one way (i.e., one switch can route 16 input links to 16 output links in one direction). We assume that hosts may be used as gateways between switches.

▷ Exercise 7.5(a)

Since there are 64 nodes, and each switch can input 16 nodes, the minimum number of switches required (assuming every node has a dedicated input to the network) is four. There are two possible designs: a single-stage recirculating network and a sequence of host/switch pairs. Figure 7.2 shows the sequence of host/switch pairs.

▷ Exercise 7.6

This exercise refers to the cut-through routing calculations performed in an example. Caveat emptor: the example in question actually performs a wormhole routing calculation. In addition, the size of the switches to be used in each configurations is not explicitly given in the exercise.

The first step to solving the exercise is to decide what the maximum depth is for each of the configurations. Assuming four-input switches, the maximum depth, D_{max}, of a fat tree that interconnects n processors is given by

$$D_{max} = \lceil \log_4 n \rceil$$

Number of Processors	Maximum Fat Tree Depth	Wormhole Routing Time (μs)
64	3	1.75
256	4	2.00
1024	5	2.25

Figure 7.3: Maximum Depth of a Fat Tree and Wormhole Routing Times for Several Processor Configurations.

where we take the ceiling[1] of the right-hand side of this equation because switches come in integral quantities. A fat tree with n-input switches can be viewed as multiple n-ary trees,[2] the maximum depth of each being $\log_n N$ where N is the number of leaves in the tree.

Given the depths of the fat trees in each case we can solve the exercise. Assuming the transfer time, transfer rate, and switch times are the same as those used in the example on page 594 (1μs) we can compute the time for wormhole routing:

$$Routing\ Time = (Switches \times Switch\ Delay) + Transfer\ Time$$

Using this equation in conjunction with the depths outlined above yields the results shown in Figure 7.3. As we would expect, the routing time increases as the number of processors increases. However, the time does not increase nearly as fast as the number of processing elements increases!

▷ Exercise 7.9

This exercise considers a fat tree like that shown in Figure 7.14 in the text but with half as many processors. However, the exercise does not specify whether you are to use the same size switches as Figure 7.14. The results of the comparison may differ if you elect to implement the fat tree with smaller switches in order to make the switch size consistent with the other interconnects being examined.

In each of the systems we consider, there are eight processing elements connected through one of three types of networks. The interconnection networks

---

[1]We define the ceiling of x, written $\lceil x \rceil$, as the largest integer y such that $y \geq x$.

[2]In an n-ary tree, each node has exactly n children.

Network Type	Best Case (cycles)	Worst Case (cycles)	P0 → P6 (cycles)	P1 → P7 (cycles)
Crossbar	1	1	1	1
Omega	3	3	3	3
Fat Tree	1	3	3	3

Figure 7.4: Latency of Several Interconnection Networks.

considered in this example include (illustrated in Figures 7.13 and 7.14 of the text)

- *Crossbar:* Processing elements (PEs) are at most one switch away from any other PE.

- *Omega:* For eight PEs, this network allows each PE to be exactly three switches away from all other PEs.

- *Fat tree:* The number of switches varies as the "distance" between the PEs changes.

Figure 7.4 presents various communication times in cycles assuming the formats shown in the text. For the most part, these answers should be clear by looking at the figures in the text and recalling that we assume a message takes one cycle to pass through a switch. In arriving at these times, we assume that the message does not have any competition for the switches during its transition through the network. Also, for the fat tree we assume it is built out of four-input switches. This serves to skew the comparison with the omega network, which only uses two-input switches. Reducing the size of the switch adds additional levels of switching, which will only impact the worst case time.

While the crossbar and omega networks both provide consistent latencies regardless of the routing, there can be differences in the fat tree latencies based on the source and destination of the routing. This should be obvious from Figure 7.14. One of the nice features of fat trees is that messages between local processing elements do not have to work all the way into the network to be handled (e.g., compare the paths between P0 and P1 with the paths between P0 and P15 in Figure 7.14). It is this feature that makes the best and worst case times different. In a network such as the omega, a message must work all the way through each of the three stages before being delivered.

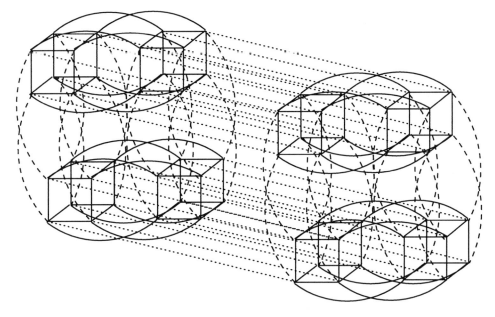

Figure 7.5: Drawing of Binary 6-Cube.

▷ **Exercise 7.12**

This question asks us to show a drawing of a binary 6-cube using a drawing like that in Figure 7.16 in the text. To make a *d*-cube, the pattern is to create two $(d-1)$-cubes and connect the corresponding vertices of the two lower order cubes. Doing so leads to the drawing shown in Figure 7.5.

▷ **Exercise 7.13**

M/M/1 queues are discussed both in Section 6.4 and in an example in Section 7.5 on page 592. Further, we make the assumption that the interarrival times are exponentially distributed to cut down on the hairy math.

To solve these exercises, we apply the formulas developed in Chapter 6 for an M/M/1 queue to the network gateway under consideration. The number of tasks in a system is given by Little's Law:

$$Length = Arrival\ Rate \times Response\ Time \qquad (7.2)$$

Next, the utilization is given by

$$Utilization = \frac{Arrival\ Rate}{Service\ Rate} \tag{7.3}$$

Finally, the time spent in the queue is given by

$$Time_{queue} = Time_{server} \times \frac{Utilization}{1 - Utilization} \tag{7.4}$$

assuming the interarrival times are exponentially distributed.

▷ Exercise 7.13(a)

Using Equation 7.3, which relates the utilization of a queuing system to the arrival rate and service rate, we can find the utilization of the gateway:

$$
\begin{aligned}
Utilization &= \frac{Arrival\ Rate}{Service\ Rate} = Arrival\ Rate \times Service\ Time \\
&= \left(200s^{-1}\right) \times \left(2 \times 10^{-3}s\right) = 40\%
\end{aligned}
$$

where the service time is defined as the inverse of the service rate. In this situation, the gateway is utilized only 40% of the time.

▷ Exercise 7.13(c)

The average time in the gateway is the sum of the time spent in the system and the time spent in the queue. Using Equation 7.4 for the time spent in the queue and 2ms from the exercise statement as the time spent in the system leads to

$$
\begin{aligned}
Time_{gateway} &= Time_{queue} + Time_{system} \\
&= \left(2\text{ms} \times \frac{40\%}{1 - 40\%}\right) + 2\text{ms} = 3.3\text{ms}
\end{aligned}
$$

Thus, on average it takes a packet 3.3ms to move through the gateway.

Chapter 8

Multiprocessors

Introduction to the Chapter 8 Exercises

The final chapter in the text explores issues relating to multiprocessor systems. Chapter 8 begins by describing some of the different types of parallelism we can find in applications and the issues that arise in centralized and distributed shared-memory architectures. The chapter closes with a discussion of memory consistency models, synchronization, and cross-cutting issues. For the case study, the SGI Challenge multiprocessor is analyzed.

▷ Exercise 8.1

To solve this exercise, we compute the amount of time spent in the "half the processors in use" mode on the *enhanced* system. We begin by defining t_{up} as the time the application requires on a uniprocessor (i.e., all code is executed serially) and t_{mp} as the time the application requires on a multiprocessor. From the exercise statement we know that

$$
t_{up} = (F_{serial}t_{mp}) + (S_{half}F_{half}t_{mp}) + (S_{all}F_{all}t_{mp})
$$
$$
\frac{t_{up}}{t_{mp}} = (F_{serial}) + (S_{half}F_{half}) + (S_{all}F_{all})
$$

where F_i is the fraction of time the multiprocessor system spends in mode i, and S_i is the speedup in mode i. Note that the ratio of the execution times on the right-hand side of the final equation is simply the speedup. Essentially, we use the total multiprocessor times and fractions in conjunction with the speedups to determine the time it would take on a uniprocessor system. In

117

this exercise, we are interested in determining the largest value of F_{half} that allows for a speedup of 80 over a uniprocessor.

From the exercise statement we know that F_{serial} is 0.02%. With this information we can derive an expression for F_{all} in terms of F_{half}:

$$
\begin{aligned}
1 &= F_{serial} + F_{half} + F_{all} \\
F_{all} &= 1 - 0.02\% - F_{half} \\
&= 0.9998 - F_{half}
\end{aligned}
$$

Finally, this result along with the speedups from the exercise can be plugged into the above result for the ratio of the uniprocessor and multiprocessor times:

$$
\begin{aligned}
\frac{t_{up}}{t_{mp}} &= 0.02\% + 50F_{half} + 100\left(99.98\% - F_{half}\right) \\
80 &= 0.02\% + 50F_{half} + 99.98 - 100F_{half} \\
F_{half} &= 39.96\%
\end{aligned}
$$

Thus, half the processors can be used at most 40% of the time on the enhanced system if we are to obtain a speedup of 80 over a uniprocessor.

▷ Exercise 8.5

An obvious complication introduced by providing a valid bit per word is the need to match not only the tag of the line but also the offset within the line when snooping the bus. In addition, the cache must be changed to support writebacks of partial cache blocks. When writing back a block, only those words that are valid should be written to memory as the contents of invalid words are not necessarily coherent with the system. Finally, given that the state machine described in Figure 8.12 of the text is applied at *each* cache block we must find a way to allow this diagram to apply to our case, where the state can be different from word to word within the block. The easiest way to deal with this problem would be to provide the state information for each word within a block. However, doing so would require much more than one valid bit per word. Without this replication of information, the only solution is to change the coherence protocol slightly.

▷ Exercise 8.7

These questions ask us to compare a hybrid DSM configuration with the central shared-memory design of the SGI Power Challenge.

▷ Exercise 8.7(b)

Letting PC stand for the Power Challenge configuration, and DPC the new hybrid Power Challenge, we make the following observations:

1. On PC, local and remote misses cost the same number of cycles since there is only one kind of non-cache memory.

2. On DPC, a miss to local memory takes 75 clocks (given in the exercise statement), while a miss to remote memory takes 164 clocks (from Exercise 8.7(a)).

The data from Ocean states that 3% of the references miss to local memory, while 1% miss to remote memory. We assume that all "hits" are to L1 cache since we do not know the difference in latency between L1 and L2. We also assume the time to hit L1 cache is 2 cycles since this is also unspecified. Thus, the average memory access time on the hybrid version of the Power Challenge is

$$
\begin{aligned}
AMAT_{DPC} &= (\%\ Hits \times Hit\ Cost) + \\
&\quad (\%\ Hits\ to\ Local\ Memory \times Time\ for\ Local\ Ref) + \\
&\quad (\%\ Remote\ Accesses \times 164) \\
&= (96\% \times 2) + (3\% \times 75) + (1\% \times 164) \\
&= 5.81
\end{aligned}
$$

and the average memory access time on the original Power Challenge is

$$
\begin{aligned}
AMAT_{PC} &= (\%\ Hits \times Hit\ Cost) + (\%\ Misses \times 164) \\
&= (96\% \times 2) + (4\% \times 164) \\
&= 8.48
\end{aligned}
$$

▷ Exercise 8.9

This questions asks us to consider a DSM design that is based on a mesh interconnect rather than on a bus. The idea behind such a design is that local accesses will be faster than a pure shared-memory approach since accesses to local memory do not need to go across a shared bus. Additionally, the cost of a remote access will be a function of start up time and number of hops across the network rather than the time to acquire the bus.

We will use the abbreviations PC for Power Challenge and DPC for distributed memory Power Challenge.

▷ Exercise 8.9(a)

The cost of local references is easy to compute. For the PC, using the same values as on pages 730–731 in the text, local references require 40 clocks to detect L2 miss, 66 clocks to deliver the data, and 58 clocks to reload caches, yielding a total of 164 clocks.

For the DPC, it requires 40 clocks to detect the L2 miss, 150ns (or 22.5 clocks) to deliver the data (as specified in the exercise statement), and 58 clocks to reload the caches, yielding a total of 120.5 clocks.

▷ Exercise 8.9(b)

For this part of the exercise, we are asked to factor in the cost of references that need to travel across the mesh network and to compute the average remote memory access time (ARMAT). Since network clocks and processor clocks take different amounts of time, we refer to network clocks as nclks and processor clocks as pclks. From the text, we already know that the cost on the PC is 164pclks or 1094ns.

For the DPC, because the result depends on how one measures the average number of hops that a reference must make in the network, we will make the simple assumption that each remote reference must make on average 1.5 hops in the X direction and 1.5 hops in the Y direction to get to its target node and so the total average distance is 3 hops.

For the complete request on the DPC, the following times must be added together: the time for the L2 miss to be recognized locally, the startup time for the message, the time for the address request to go across the network (assume only 32 bits are needed for this message), the time for the remote memory to respond (150ns), the time for the data to return across the network (a 128-byte cache line), and the time for the caches to be reloaded.

The time across the network is based on the number of hops and the size of the message. We are given that 2 bytes can be sent every nclk, and so the time to pass through a switch is

$$Time \ to \ Send \ = \ \frac{Number \ of \ Bytes}{2 \ bytes \ per \ nclk} \tag{8.1}$$

Putting this into an equation yields

$$
\begin{aligned}
ARMAT \ = \ & 40 \ pclks \ + \\
& 5 \ nclks \ + \\
& 2 \ nclks + (3 \times 1 \ nclks) \ + \\
& 150\text{ns} \ + \\
& 64 \ nclks + (3 \times 1 \ nclks) \ + \\
& 58 \ pclks \\
= \ & 1574\text{ns}
\end{aligned}
$$

To compute the point at which the machines' performance will cross over (considering percent of remote misses), only requires that we compare the average cost when a reference does not hit in cache (since all other costs are the same). From Exercise 8.9(a), we know the cost of a cache miss satisfied by local memory on the DPC is 120.5pclks or 803ns.

$$
\begin{aligned}
Miss \ Cost_{DPC} \ = \ & (\% \ Local \ Cache \ Misses \times 803\text{ns}) \ + \\
& [(1 - \% \ Local \ Cache \ Misses) \times 1574\text{ns}] \\
Miss \ Cost_{PC} \ = \ & 1094\text{ns}
\end{aligned}
$$

Solving for % *Local Cache Miss* yields a value of 62%. Thus, at least 62% of the cache misses must be satisfied locally on the DPC for its performance to exceed the performance of the PC.

▷ Exercise 8.13

There is no Ocean data for 32 processors in text Figure 8.13 as stated in the question. We use 16-processor data for this solution instead.

This question is asking for the cutoff point between the COMA and DSM configurations given the behavior and cost of capacity and coherence misses for each machine. Coherence misses for both machines cost 100 clocks. For the COMA machine, a capacity miss costs 50 clocks and always hits in local memory. For the DSM machine, a capacity miss costs 40 cycles if local and 75 cycles otherwise. According to the Ocean data 2% of the misses will be coherence and 7% will be capacity.

We assume that all types of memory references not specifically mentioned cost the same on both architectures. To compute the portion of capacity misses that must be local for the DSM to have the same performance as the COMA we must set the formula for time spent satisfying coherence and capacity misses for each system equal and solve.

Let L be the fraction of misses that are local and R the fraction that are remote. Therefore,

$$
\begin{aligned}
Miss\ Time_{COMA} &= (0.07 \times 50) + (0.02 \times 100) \\
Miss\ Time_{DSM} &= \{0.07 \times [(L \times 40) + (R \times 75)]\} + (0.02 \times 100)
\end{aligned}
$$

and note that

$$1 = L + R \tag{8.2}$$

If we set the two miss times equal to each other and simplify, we get

$$3.5 = (2.8 \times L) + (5.25 \times R) \tag{8.3}$$

Solving for L and R in Equations 8.2 and 8.3 yields

$$
\begin{aligned}
L &= 0.71 \\
R &= 0.29
\end{aligned}
$$

▷ Exercise 8.23

As this exercise does not identify the amount of time a processor requires to read the release flag, we consider the time to synchronize to be the time for all processors to arrive at the barrier. We also ignore cache coherence overhead. Finally, we assume that the counters at each node of the tree can be accessed simultaneously.

A k-ary tree is a tree where each non-leaf node has k children. The depth,[1] D, of such a tree is given by

$$D = \log_k n$$

where n is the number of leaves in the tree. In this solution, we assume that n is an integral power of k.

In the combining tree barrier, each non-leaf node in the tree corresponds to a unique barrier with its own counter. Synchronization takes place at each non-leaf node in the tree and moves from the leaves up through the D levels to the root. As the tree is k-ary, the barriers at each non-leaf node synchronize at most k incoming requests. Consider what occurs when we begin the barrier synchronization. First, k things each spend c cycles contending for the counter and one thing is granted access while $k-1$ things are turned away. Next, the remaining $k-1$ things repeat the same process with fewer and fewer things contending for the counter as time goes by. Therefore, the total number of cycles required to synchronize a node of the combining tree barrier is given by

$$\sum_{i=0}^{k-1} (k-i)\, c = \frac{k\,(k-1)\,c}{2}$$

In arriving at this expression, we assume that all of the things contending for access to the counter generate a bus request which requires c cycles to satisfy.

The levels within the tree synchronize serially, as level i must wait for level $i+1$ to synchronize. Thus, the total time to synchronize is

$$t_{sync} = \sum_{i=1}^{\log_k n} \frac{k\,(k-1)\,c}{2} = \left[\frac{k\,(k-1)\,c}{2}\right] \log_k n$$

This result can be derived by noting that as each non-leaf node uses its own counter, each level can synchronize in at most $\frac{1}{2} k\,(k-1)\,c$ cycles (assuming that the synchronizations on a given level can occur simultaneously) and that there are $\log_k n$ levels of the tree that synchronize in turn.

---

[1] Here we consider the depth to be the length of the longest path between the root and any leaf.

Appendix A

Computer Arithmetic

Introduction to the Appendix A Exercises

The first appendix in the text presents an in-depth exploration of computer arithmetic. It begins by examining the basics of integer and floating-point arithmetic before moving on to techniques that can be applied to improve the performance of computer arithmetic. The appendix closes with an examination of the floating-point units on several different chips.

A number of the solutions presented in this chapter are based on answers from the solutions manual from the first edition of the book in the cases where the first and second editions use the same questions.

▷ Exercise A.3

To solve this exercise, we simply apply the rules for multiplication presented on page A–3 of the text as modified on page A–9 of the text to handle Booth recoding. Multiplying −8 by −8 using four-bit binary numbers leads to the result shown in Figure A.1. In this figure, the subscripts of a in the comments column refer to the bits in the *original* value of A, not the value currently shown in the A column. Also, remember that we must keep track of the sign of the result of an add or subtract to P to shift the correct value into the most-significant bit of P in a shift operation.

P	**A**	**Step**	**Comment**
0000	1000		Put $-8 = 1000_2$ into A and B.
0000	1000	1(i)	$a_0 = a_{-1} = 0$; $P = P + 0$ by Rule I.
0000	0100	1(ii)	Shift.
0000	0100	2(i)	$a_1 = a_0 = 0$; $P = P + 0$ by Rule I.
0000	0010	2(ii)	Shift.
0000	0010	3(i)	$a_2 = a_1 = 0$; $P = P + 0$ by Rule I.
0000	0001	3(ii)	Shift.
+ 1000		4(i)	$a_3 = 1, a_2 = 0$; $P = P - B$ by Rule III.
1000	0001		
0100	0000	4(ii)	Shift.
0100	0000		Final result is $64 = 01000000_2$

Figure A.1: Numerical Example of Booth Recoding.

▷ Exercise A.4

If we represent the equation as $X - Y = Z$ where x_i is the ith bit position of X, then a borrow happens only if $x_i - y_i - b_i < 0$. If the above relationship is written as a truth table and simplified, we get

$$b_{i+1} = \overline{x_i}(y_i + b_i) + x_i y_i b_i$$

For the result bits, $z_i = (x_i - y_i - b_i) \bmod 2$ yielding

$$z_i = \overline{x_i y_i} b_i + \overline{x_i} y_i \overline{b_i} + x_i \overline{y_i}\,\overline{b_i} + x_i \overline{y_i} b_i$$

▷ Exercise A.6

This exercise asks for simple conversions to 32-bit IEEE floating-point format.

▷ Exercise A.6(b)

$$10.5_{10} = 0\ \ 1000000010\ \ 0101000000000000000000000_2$$

▷ Exercise A.7

In these exercises, we explore various numbers as represented in the IEEE floating-point standard discussed in Section A.3 of the text.

▷ Exercise A.7(a)

Normal numbers are of the form $\pm 1.f \times 2^e$. The largest such positive number less than 1 occurs when the fraction, f, is its largest value and the exponent, e, is -1. For single precision the value we are after is

$$
\begin{aligned}
N_{binary} &= 1.11111111111111111111111_2 \times 2^{-1} \\
N_{ieee} &= 0\ 01111101\ 11111111111111111111111_2 \\
N_{decimal} &= 0.99999994 \times 10^0
\end{aligned}
$$

in the three formats.

▷ Exercise A.7(b)

Normal numbers are of the form $\pm 1.f \times 2^e$. The largest such positive number, which is also the largest number, occurs when the fraction, f, is its largest value and the exponent, e, is its largest positive value. For single precision the value we are after is

$$
\begin{aligned}
N_{binary} &= 1.11111111111111111111111_2 \times 2^{127} \\
N_{ieee} &= 0\ 11111110\ 11111111111111111111111_2 \\
N_{decimal} &= 3.402823 \times 10^{38}
\end{aligned}
$$

in the three formats.

▷ Exercise A.11

In this exercise we examine the hardware used to handle the addition of exponents in a floating-point multiplier.

▷ Exercise A.11(a)

To add the exponents in a floating-point multiply we must sum the two exponents, e_1 and e_2, and then subtract the bias, 127_{10}. In addition, rounding the exponent up or down by one may be necessary depending on how

```
if (e1 + e2) > 254 ) {
    /* overflow occurs */
} else if ( e1 + e2 == 254 ) {
    Let Fr = fraction product after shifting/rounding

    /* x0 bit in text figure A.10 */
    if ( high-order-bit(Fr) == 1 ) {
        /* overflow occurs */
    }
}
```

Figure A.2: Overflow Algorithm.

the multiply works out. The exponent addition hardware could be implemented by cascading two adders: one that performs $e_1 + e_2$, and another that performs $(e_1 + e_2) - 127_{10}$.

▷ Exercise A.12

These exercises explore the detection of overflow for floating-point multiplications.

▷ Exercise A.12(a)

For this solution, the high-level code presented in Figure A.2 provides the semantics needed to determine overflow using 9-bit adders. Since the sum of the two exponents is guaranteed to be less than $255 + 255 = 510$, 9 bits is sufficient.

▷ Exercise A.14

If we use the following denormalized IEEE floating-point single precision number:

$$X = 0 \ 00000000 \ 01000000000000000000000_2$$

and the non-denormalized floating-point number:

$$Y = 0 \ 10000010 \ 00000000000000000000000_2$$

then adding the two exponents from these numbers yields 10000010_2 and multiplying the two fractions yields $01000000000000000000000_2$ to yield the new (non-denormalized) floating-point number:

$$X \times Y = 0 \ \ 10000000 \ \ 00000000000000000000000_2$$

Since the results of the fractional multiply was 0.01_2, it requires 2 bits of shifting.

Double precision has 53 bits of precision, and at least one of those bits must be non-zero in a denormal number (otherwise, the number would be 0). In the worst case, if only the least significant bit in the 53-bit fractional results field was on (after rounding), then the result would have to be shifted as many as 53 bits to properly adjust the exponent.

▷ Exercise A.20

In these exercises, we explore iterative square root algorithms.

▷ Exercise A.20(a)

To find an iterative algorithm for the square root function, we begin by recasting the square root as finding the zero of a function. Consider taking the square root of a. To recast the square root such that Newton's algorithm can be applied, we need to find a function, $f(x)$, such that $f(x)$ is zero when x is $\sqrt{a}$. Therefore, the function we are after is

$$f(x) = x^2 - a \tag{A.1}$$

We take the derivative of Equation A.1:

$$f'(x) = 2x \tag{A.2}$$

With expressions for $f(x)$ and $f'(x)$ we can find an expression for the next "guess" in Newton's algorithm using Equation A.6.1 from the text:

$$x_{i+1} = x_i - \frac{f(x)}{f'(x)} = x_i - \frac{x_i^2 - a}{2x_i} = \frac{1}{2}\left(x_i + \frac{a}{x_i}\right) \tag{A.3}$$

where the subscript i indicates the iteration.

▷ **Exercise A.20(b)**

Recall that a floating-point number in IEEE format is expressed as the product of a significand and a power of two, $a \times 2^b$. We divide by two amounts to reduce the exponent by one:

$$\frac{a \times 2^b}{2} = a \times 2^{b-1}$$

Thus, for IEEE floating point, we could simply subtract the base two number: $000000001000\ldots000_2$ from the number to be divided. This reduces the exponent of the number to be divided by one, which serves to divide by two. Note that to apply this technique we have to be make sure the exponent does not overflow.

▷ **Exercise A.20(c)**

The expression given in the exercise for $f(x)$ has a zero at $\frac{1}{\sqrt{a}}$. Thus, using Newton's algorithm to solve this function produces the following result after n iterations:

$$x_n \approx \frac{1}{\sqrt{a}}$$

We multiply both sides by a:

$$a x_n \approx \frac{a}{\sqrt{a}} \approx \sqrt{a}$$

Thus, provided x_n can be computed without divisions, it is possible to compute the square root with Newton's algorithm without divisions.

The derivative of the expression for $f(x)$ is given by

$$f'(x) = \frac{-2}{x^3} \tag{A.4}$$

With expressions for $f(x)$ and $f'(x)$ we can find an expression for the next "guess" in Newton's algorithm using Equation A.6.1 from the text:

$$x_{i+1} = x_i - \frac{f(x)}{f'(x)} = x_i - \frac{\frac{1}{x_i^2} - a}{-\frac{2}{x_i^3}} = \frac{x_i}{2}\left(3 - a x_i^2\right) \tag{A.5}$$

where the subscript i indicates the iteration.

▷ Exercise A.21

These exercises concern mathematical properties of iterative division algorithms.

▷ Exercise A.21(a)

Since x is between 1 and 2, the most significant bits in the significand are $\frac{1}{2}$, $\frac{1}{4}$, etc. Thus, the least significant bit in the significant is 2^{1-p}, and values within the range of 1 to 2 can be incremented by 2^{1-p}, yielding

$$x + 2^{1-p}$$

▷ Exercise A.21(b)

Since $\overline{q}$ has a few extra bits of precision, we are asked to provide a $p+1$ bit precision number based on that value. First, truncate $\overline{q}$ to $p+1$ bits and add 2^{-p}. To show this quantity is precise to $p+1$ bits, we need to show that

$$|q - q'| < 2^{-p}$$

Notice the following sequence of relations:

$$\overline{q} - 2^{-p} \le trunc\,(\overline{q}) \le \overline{q}$$
$$\overline{q} \le trunc\,(\overline{q}) + 2^{-p} \le \overline{q} + 2^{-p}$$
$$\overline{q} \le q' \le \overline{q} + 2^{-p}$$

Since by hypothesis, $\overline{q} \le q < \overline{q} + 2^{-p}$, both q and q' are between $\overline{q}$ and $\overline{q} + 2^{-p}$, implying that $|q' - q| \le 2^{-p}$

To show that the difference is strictly less than, we proceed by contradiction. Suppose $|q' - q| = 2^{-p}$. Then q has a significand that is a multiple of 2^{-p}. This implies that because $\overline{q} < q$, $trunc\,(\overline{q}) = q - 2^{-p}$ and so $q' = q$, which contradicts the supposition. Thus, $|q' - q| < 2^{-p}$.

▷ Exercise A.27

In these exercises, we explore how a carry-lookahead tree can be implemented by refining the circuitry presented in Figures A.15, A.17, and A.18 of the text.

▷ **Exercise A.27(a)**

Box 1 of Figure A.15 in the text is responsible for determining the values of the carry generate, g_i, and carry propagate, p_i, signals for bit i of the computation. There are four possible cases:

1. $a_i = 0, b_i = 0$: Bit i of the sum will neither generate nor propagate a carry in this case. Both g_i and p_i should be 0.

2. $a_i = 0, b_i = 1$: Bit i of the sum will propagate, but not generate, a carry in this case. Therefore, g_i should be 0 and p_i should be 1.

3. $a_i = 1, b_i = 0$: This case is the same as case 2.

4. $a_i = 1, b_i = 1$: Bit i of the sum always generates a carry regardless of the carry-in. Therefore, g_i should be 1 and p_i should be 0.

These cases can be derived by considering how the carry-out is generated when a_i, b_i, and the carry-in are added.

From Figure A.15, we know that Box 1 takes a_i and b_i as inputs to generate g_i and p_i. Therefore, the circuitry in Box 1 implements the following logic functions:

$$
\begin{aligned}
g_i &= a_i b_i \\
p_i &= a_i + b_i
\end{aligned}
$$

Drawing the actual gates is left as an exercise for the reader.[1]

Box 2 of Figure A.15 combines the generate and propagate signals from two bits to form a "level" in the carry-lookahead tree. This box implements the relationships for G_{ik} and P_{ik} presented in Equations A.8.5 and A.8.6 on page A–40 of the text. Therefore, the circuitry in Box 2 implements the following logic functions:

$$
\begin{aligned}
G_{ik} &= G_{j+1,k} + P_{j+1,k} G_{ij} \\
P_{ik} &= P_{ij} P_{j+1,k}
\end{aligned}
$$

Again, drawing the actual gates is left as an exercise for the reader.

---

[1] I've always wanted to say that...

▷ **Exercise A.28**

To solve this exercise, we simply need to determine a relationship between the binary value of bits $i-1$, i, and $i+1$ that generates the appropriate multiple, m of b. Our search is greatly aided by Figure A.25 of the text, which outlines the relationship we are looking for. For example, we would like a function, $f(a_{i-1}, a_i, a_{i+1})$ that has the value $+2$ when $a_{i-1} = a_i = 1$ and $a_{i+1} = 0$. Such a function is

$$f(a_{i-1}, a_i, a_{i+1}) = a_{i-1} + a_i - 2a_{i+1}$$

Appendix B

Vector Processors

Introduction to the Appendix B Exercises

Appendix B explores techniques used by vector machines to exploit instruction level parallelism. These techniques rely on the properties of vectors both to reduce the instruction bandwidth and increase the amount of parallelism available in the code stream. After providing a motivation for using vector techniques, the text presents a version of DLX, called DLXV, that is extended to support vector operations. DLXV serves as a model to explore the performance of vector processors and means by which their performance can be improved. The appendix concludes with a discussion of a few of the common performance metrics applied to vector systems.

Convoys, Chimes, and Cycles

Several of the exercises in this appendix utilize convoys, chimes, and cycles to estimate performance of vector code sequences. Before presenting the solutions, it is helpful to discuss some of the common features of these performance analysis exercises. As discussed in the text, there are two factors to consider when grouping instructions into convoys:

- The instructions in a convoy may not create structural hazards when executing simultaneously.

- The instructions in a convoy may not have data dependences.

The second condition can be relaxed by implementing chaining. With chaining, instructions with data dependences that reside in the same convoy can share results.

To evaluate the number of clock cycles required by a vector sequence it is helpful to construct a table that illustrates the starting, first-result, and last-result times of each convoy in the vector sequence being evaluated. An example of such a table can be found in Figure B.5 of the text. The times in these tables include

- *Starting Time:* The cycle in which the convoy begins execution, which is simply the cycle following the last result time of the previous convoy.

- *First-Result Time:* The cycle in which the first result of the convoy is produced. This time accounts for a period of start-up overhead, which the vector unit spends filling its pipeline. Assuming a vector unit with a start-up overhead of p produces its first result $p + 1$ cycles after starting;[1] the first-result time is the starting time plus the start-up overhead for the convoy plus one. Throughout these solutions we use the start-up overheads shown in Figure B.6 of the text.

- *Last-Result Time:* The cycle in which the final result of the convoy is produced. Using the definition of start-up overhead above and assuming a vector length of n, the convoy produces $n - 1$ results in the succeeding cycles after producing its first result. Therefore, the last-result time is the first-result time plus the length of the vector the convoy operates on minus one.

The time to complete the entire sequence can then be found from the time the last convoy in the sequence produces its last result.

Several assumptions should be mentioned at this point. First, the last-result time makes the reasonable assumption that in steady-state a vector unit produces one result per clock cycle. Also, our definition of the first-result time assumes that a vector unit with a start-up overhead of p produces its first result $p + 1$ cycles after the computation begins. We are essentially assuming that the start-up overhead represents the time that must pass before the vector unit can produce a result each clock cycle. Finally, the start-up overhead used to determine the first-result time depends on whether or not instructions within a convoy are chained and on the "structure" of the convoy.

When several choices exist for the start-up overhead, we select the overhead that provides the latest final-result time for the convoy, as succeeding

---

[1] In our solutions, we define the overhead to be the time that must pass *before* the vector unit can *begin* producing one result per cycle.

convoys can not begin execution before this point. When instructions are not chained, the start-up overhead is the largest of the overheads of the individual instructions because the overheads can be overlapped during execution. When instructions are chained, the overheads of each instruction in the chain must be added together, because a result passes through each vector unit in the chain. In convoys with a combination of chained and unchained operations, the largest of the overhead of the unchained operations and the overhead of chained groups of operations must be selected.

The table technique outlined above works well when the code is not being strip mined. When strip mining is being utilized for vector lengths longer than the native vector lengths, the expression for T_n developed in Section B.3 can be applied:[2]

$$T_n = \left\lceil \frac{n}{MVL} \right\rceil (T_{loop} + T_{start}) + nT_{chime}$$

T_n represents the time to execute the vector sequence on a vector of length n when the native vector length of the machine is MVL. Note that T_n produces the same times as those in a table such as Figure B.5 when $n \leq MVL$.

▷ Exercise B.2

These exercises explore the execution of a simple DLXV vector sequence on several hardware configurations. After solving these exercises, you should appreciate how the addition of chaining and more memory bandwidth can improve the performance of the system. The solution strategy for each part of this exercise is the same:

- Partition the code into convoys based on the hardware configuration.

- Determine the total time to execute the vector sequence using the techniques outlined in the discussion on page 135 of this manual.

- Use the total execution time along with observations of the code to determine the number of cycles per result.

For these exercises, we elect to determine the execution times using tables such as Figure B.5 in the text rather than applying the formula for T_n. As mentioned in the introduction, we assume the start-up overheads presented in Figure B.6 of the text.

---

[2]The formula for T_n is incorrectly specified on page B–30 of the text—the "bonus" T_{base} term should be removed.

▷ Exercise B.2(a)

The first step to solving the exercise is to partition the code from the exercise into convoys. The code for Exercise B.2 can be partitioned into four convoys on a DLXV without chaining and with a single memory pipeline (i.e., vector load/store unit):

1. The LV must reside in its own convoy as it produces a result used by the next two instructions (the ADDV and the MULTV).

2. The ADDV and MULTV can be placed in the next convoy as there are no structural hazards or data dependences between them and they depend on the result of the previous convoy (the LV).

3. The first SV can not be grouped with the ADDV and MULTV due to a data dependence and therefore must be placed in a new convoy.

4. The second SV can not be grouped with the first SV because doing so causes a structural hazard for the memory pipeline. Thus, the second SV is placed in its own convoy.

The code for Exercise B.2 thus executes in 4 chimes on a DLXV with a single memory pipeline and without chaining.

To determine the number of cycles per result, we first compute the time to execute the vector sequence including start-up overhead. Using the start-up overheads shown in Figure B.6 and assuming a vector length of n leads to Figure B.1 which presents an execution profile of the code on a DLXV without chaining and with a single memory pipeline. In this figure, the first convoy begins in cycle 0 and by cycle 12 produces its first result (recall that loads have a start-up overhead of 12 cycles). Given a vector length of n, the load retrieves its last result in cycle $11 + n$. On the next cycle, $12 + n$, the second convoy begins. In this convoy, because there are two instructions with different start-up overheads that are not chained, we select the longer of the two overheads to determine when the convoy completes execution.[3] The second convoy produces its first result at cycle $12 + n + 7$ given a start-up overhead of seven cycles for the multiply and completes at cycle $(19 + n) + (n - 1)$ The ADDV finishes before this cycle as it has a shorter start-up overhead.

From Figure B.1 the last convoy produces its last result during cycle $42 + 4n$, which implies that the sequence, which started on cycle 0, takes

---

[3]See the discussion on page 135 of this manual.

Convoy	Starts	First Result	Last Result
1 LV	0	$0 + 12$	$12 + (n - 1)$
2 MULTV, ADDV	$12 + n$	$(12 + n) + 7$	$(19 + n) + (n - 1)$
3 SV	$19 + 2n$	$(19 + 2n) + 12$	$(31 + 2n) + (n - 1)$
4 SV	$31 + 3n$	$(31 + 3n) + 12$	$(43 + 3n) + (n - 1)$

Figure B.1: Execution Profile of the Code Sequence on DLXV without Chaining and with a Single Memory Pipeline.

$42 + 4n + 1$ cycles to execute. For a vector length, n, of 64, execution requires 299 cycles.[4] With both stores counting as a single result, the code sequence for this exercise produces 64 results (as the vector length is 64 and each element in **V2** or **V4** counts as a single result). Thus, the code requires $\frac{299}{64}$ or 4.7 cycles per result on this version of DLXV.

▷ Exercise B.3

The formula for T_n presented on page B–30 of the text has a T_{base} term that was used in the expression for T_n presented in the first edition of the text. T_{base} should not appear in the second edition as the authors have changed the way they compute T_n.

This exercise asks us to compute several measures of vector performance on the DLXV code for a simple FORTRAN loop. Before going into the solutions, let us review the various measurements we will use. The time to execute the code on a vector of length n, T_n, is given by the following expression derived in Section B.3 of the text:

$$T_n = \left\lceil \frac{n}{MVL} \right\rceil (T_{loop} + T_{start}) + n T_{chime} \qquad \text{(B.1)}$$

The MFLOPS rating of the vector machine, R_n, can be found by combining Equation B.1 with an expression for MFLOPs from Chapter 1:

$$
\begin{aligned}
R_n &= \frac{Operations \ per \ Iteration \times Clock \ Rate}{Clock \ Cycles \ per \ Iteration} \\[2mm]
&= \frac{Operations \ per \ Iteration \times Clock \ Rate}{\frac{1}{n} T_n} \qquad \text{(B.2)}
\end{aligned}
$$

---

[4]We could also determine this value using the expression for T_n.

```
iloop:  LV      V0, Rb          ; V0 = B(i)
        MULTSV  V1, V0, F0      ; V1 = B(i) * x
        LV      V2, Ra          ; V2 = A(i)
        ADDV    V3, V0, V2      ; V3 = A(i) + B(i)
        SV      Ra, V3          ; A(i) = A(i) + B(i)
        SV      Rb, V1          ; B(i) = x * B(i)
```

Figure B.2: A DLXV Code Sequence for the Inner Portion of the Loop.

In the final form of R_n we replace the number of clock cycles per iteration[5] with $\frac{1}{n}T_n$. By taking the limit of Equation B.2 as n goes to infinity, we can arrive at the MFLOPS rate of the code on a vector of infinite length:

$$
\begin{aligned}
R_\infty &= \lim_{n\to\infty} \left(\frac{\text{Operations per Iteration} \times \text{Clock Rate}}{\frac{1}{n}T_n} \right) \\
&= \text{Operations per Iteration} \times \text{Clock Rate} \times \left(\lim_{n\to\infty} \frac{T_n}{n} \right)^{-1} \quad \text{(B.3)}
\end{aligned}
$$

As the clock rate and number of operations per iteration are constant with respect to n, they can be moved outside of the limit.

▷ Exercise B.3(a)

Since we are considering DLXV, we assume the machine has a single memory pipeline and supports chaining (see Figure B.1 and Section B.6 of the text). The vector code for the inner portion of the FORTRAN loop is shown in Figure B.2. Because the FORTRAN loop in the exercise iterates from 1 to n, the "inner portion" shown in Figure B.2 would be surrounded by code to implement strip-mining when the vectors are longer than the native vector length.

Rather than loading both vectors before computing A(i) or B(i), we perform the MULTSV immediately after the first LV. This allows us to do some useful work while the LV is executing, since the MULTSV can be chained to the LV. If we were to perform both LVs before the MULTSV, the machine would serialize the LV instructions (since there is only one memory pipeline) and therefore not exploit some of the parallelism present in the code.

---

[5] Here, "iteration" refers to an iteration of the *source* code.

```
iloop:  LV      V0, Rb          ; convoy #1
        MULTSV  V1, V0, F0      ; convoy #1 (chained)
        LV      V2,Ra           ; convoy #2
        ADDV    V3,V0,V2        ; convoy #2 (chained)
        SV      Ra,V3           ; convoy #3
        SV      Rb,V1           ; convoy #4
```

Figure B.3: A DLXV Code Sequence for the Inner Portion of the Loop.

▷ Exercise B.3(b)

To evaluate T_n shown in Equation B.1, we need to determine the values of T_{chime} and T_{start} on the code of interest. T_{chime} is the number of convoys our code is divided into, while T_{start} is the total start-up overhead for all convoys. Figure B.3 shows how the DLXV code developed in Exercise B.3(a) for this exercise can be divided into convoys assuming the DLXV shown in Figure B.1 of the text with chaining.

As this figure has four convoys, T_{chime} is 4 for the DLXV code shown in Figure B.3. T_{start} is determined from the total start-up overhead for all of the convoys in Figure B.3 using the overheads from the text.[6]

- *Convoy 1:* Because the **MULTSV** and the first **LV** are chained, the start-up overhead is the sum of the **LV** and **MULTSV** overheads, or 19 cycles.

- *Convoy 2:* Because the **ADDV** and the second **LV** are chained, the start-up overhead is the sum of the **LV** and **ADDV** overheads, or 18 cycles.

- *Convoys 3 & 4:* Each consists of a single **SV**, which implies that the total overhead for both convoys is 24 cycles.

Therefore, T_{start} is $19 + 18 + 24$, or 61 cycles. Solving Equation B.1 leads to a value for T_{100}:

$$T_{100} = \left\lceil \frac{100}{64} \right\rceil (15 + 61) + 100\,(4) = 552$$

where we assume a value of 15 cycles for T_{loop} as specified in the exercise statement.

With a value for T_{100} we can now apply Equation B.2 to compute R_{100}:

$$R_{100} = \frac{2 \text{ FLOP} \times 200 \text{ MHz} \times 100}{552} = 72.5 \text{ MFLOPS}$$

---

[6]Figure B.6 in the text for the short-term memory challenged.

For the code used in this exercise, the number of operations per iteration is two: one for the **MULTSV** and one for the **ADDV**. The clock rate is given as 200 MHz.

▷ **Exercise B.3(d)**

$N_{1/2}$, the vector length needed to achieve one-half of R_∞, is the smallest value of n such that

$$R_n \geq \frac{1}{2} R_\infty \tag{B.4}$$

Because R_n contains a ceiling term in the expression for T_n, we will assume for the moment that the vector length is less than or equal to MVL to simplify T_n. To determine T_n, we plug the results from Exercise B.3(b) along with the assumption that $n \leq MVL$ into Equation B.1:

$$T_n = 1 \left(T_{loop} + T_{start} \right) + n T_{chime} = 4n + 76$$

which can be combined with Equation B.2 to determine R_n:

$$R_n = 2 \text{ FLOP} \times 200 \text{ MHz} \times \left(\frac{4n + 76}{n} \right)^{-1} = \frac{n \times 400 \text{ MFLOPS}}{4n + 76} \tag{B.5}$$

In this expression we utilize the results from Exercise B.3(b) for the clock rate and number of floating-point operations per iteration. Combining Equation B.4 with B.5 and solving for n leads to a value for $N_{1/2}$:

$$\frac{n \times 400 \text{ MFLOPS}}{4n + 76} \geq 38.6 \text{ MFLOPS} \quad \Rightarrow n \geq 8.8 \quad \Rightarrow N_{1/2} = 9$$

where the value of $\frac{1}{2} R_\infty$ is 38.6 MFLOPS, from the result of Exercise B.3(b). Therefore, vectors must have at least nine elements to achieve one-half the performance of that achieved on vectors of infinite length. Note that our assumption that $N_{1/2} \leq MVL$ holds under this condition.

▷ **Exercise B.4**

This exercise explores the performance of a memory system with banks on DLXV. Before solving this exercise, you may want to review the discussion of memory banks provided in Chapter 5 of the text.

Access	Address	Bank	Starts	Finishes
1	0	0	0	$0 + 8 = 8$
2	20	4	1	$1 + 8 = 9$
3	40	0	9	$9 + 8 = 17$
4	60	4	10	$10 + 8 = 18$

Figure B.4: DLXV Memory System Behavior.

▷ Exercise B.4(a)

Because we are accessing eight banks with a stride of 20, the possible addresses only map onto two different banks. Figure B.4 illustrates the behavior of the first several accesses. Although this figure assumes the accesses begin at address 0, this assumption is not necessary to solve the problem. Changing the starting address will cause the two banks hit by the references to change but otherwise will not affect the answer.

From Figure B.4 the first two accesses take $8 + 1 + 1 = 10$ cycles to complete. The remaining 62 accesses take $8 + 1 + 1 - 2 = 8$ cycles for each pair (note that the -2 term comes from overlap between a given pair and the immediately preceding and succeeding pair). This gives a total of $10 + \frac{62}{2} \times 8 = 258$ cycles.

▷ Exercise B.5

This exercise explores the *loop fission* optimization that allows a loop with a dependence to be partially vectorized. This is accomplished by splitting the loop into a dependence-free portion (which can be vectorized) and a remainder that has a dependence (which can not be vectorized).

▷ Exercise B.5(a)

To perform *loop fission*, we will split the loop given in the exercise into two parts: one without a dependence, and one with a dependence. The FORTRAN for the transformed loop is shown in Figure B.5. Note that there are no dependences in the first loop of this code, while the second loop has a loop-carried dependence on C (i.e., the value of C at iteration i depends on the value of C from iteration i-1).

```
         do 10 i = 1, 64
             A(i) = A(i) + B(i)
  10         continue
         C = 0.0
         do 20 i = 1, 64
             C = C + A(i)
  20         continue
```

Figure B.5: FORTRAN Loop after the Application of Loop Fission.

▷ Exercise B.6

The formula for T_n presented on page B–30 of the text has a T_{base} term that was used in the expression for T_n presented in the first edition of the text. T_{base} should not appear in the second edition as the authors have changed the way they compute T_n.

These exercises illustrate how compiler improvements can lead to large performance gains. We begin by generating the "obvious" vector code to implement a FORTRAN loop and measuring its performance. Next, by improving the vector code we examine how the performance can be improved if the compiler is smarter about how it generates code. In exploring the performance, we use the expression for the time to execute the code on a vector of length n, T_n, given by the following expression:

$$T_n = \left\lceil \frac{n}{MVL} \right\rceil (T_{loop} + T_{start}) + nT_{chime} \tag{B.6}$$

This equation is derived in Section B.3 of the text.

▷ Exercise B.6(a)

The straightforward code to implement the inner loop of the FORTRAN source is shown in Figure B.6. This code sequence represents the inner `do` loop in the FORTRAN source, which processes elements along the `j` direction. This vector code would be enclosed in additional scalar code to move along the `i` direction for the outer `do` loop.

▷ Exercise B.6(b)

This exercise provides enough information to estimate the performance of the entire FORTRAN code sequence. Although not

```
simple: LV      V1, X(i)        ; load row i of X(i,j)
        MULTSV  V2, Fa, V1      ; form a*X(i,j)
        LV      V3, Y(k)        ; load row k of Y(k,j)
        ADDV    V4, V2, V3      ; form a*X(i,j) + Y(k,j)
        SV      Y(k), V4        ; save result
```

Figure B.6: A Code Sequence.

explicitly requested, we compute this time in the solution.

The first step to complete before we can determine the timing is to partition the vector code from Exercise B.6(a) into convoys. The code for this exercise, presented in Figure B.6, can be partitioned into three convoys on a DLXV with chaining and with a single memory pipeline (i.e., vector load/store unit):

1. The results of the LV are chained to the MULTSV. As chaining "eliminates" the data dependence with respect to determining convoy membership and there are no structural hazards, these three instructions can share a convoy.

2. The second LV can not be grouped with the first LV due to a structural hazard for the memory pipeline. The results of the second LV are chained to the ADDV, which allows them to share their own convoy.

3. The SV can not be grouped with either LV because doing so causes a structural hazard for the memory pipeline. Thus, the SV is placed in its own convoy.

Thus, the code for this exercise executes in three chimes on a DLXV with a single memory pipeline and chaining.

From the exercise statement and Equation B.6 we can compute the time to execute this vector code on a vector of length 64:

$$T_{64} = \left\lceil \frac{64}{64} \right\rceil (15 + 49) + 64\,(3) = 256$$

where T_{start} is given by the sum of the start-up overheads of each convoy, $(12 + 7) + (12 + 6) + 12$ or 49 cycles. This result represents the time to execute the inner loop of the FORTRAN code once. The total time can be computed from the time to execute the inner loop as follows:

$$T_{all} = i\,(T_{loop} + T_{64}) = 64\,(15 + 256) = 17.34 \times 10^3$$

```
vmloop: LD      F0, #0.0        ; F0 = 0.0
        LV      V0, Ra          ; V0 = A vector
        LV      V1, Rb          ; V1 = B vector
        SNESV   F0, V1          ; VM(i) = 1
                                ;   iff V1(i) != F0
        DIVV    V0, V0, V1      ; V0(i) = V0(i) / V1(i)
                                ;   iff VM(i) = 1
        SV      Ra, V0          ; A(i) = V0(i)
                                ;   iff VM(i) = 1
        CVM                     ; clear VM to 1's
```

Figure B.7: DLXV Code Utilizing Vector Masks to Implement a FORTRAN Loop.

which is the number of iterations of the outer loop, i, multiplied by the execution time of the body of the outer loop (T_{loop} cycles for overhead and T_{64} cycles to execute the inner loop). From the results for T_{64} and T_{all}, one can conclude that the number of chimes is the primary limitation on performance.

▷ Exercise B.7

This exercise explores the use of vector masks and scatter-gather operations to implement "conditional" operations on elements of a vector. After developing code for both approaches, the performance of the two methods is compared using the T_n vector performance measure.

▷ Exercise B.7(a)

The DLXV code shown in Figure B.7 implements the FORTRAN code snippet using DLXV's vector-mask capability. In this code, we set the vector-mask register, VM, to be 1 where $B(i) \neq 0$ and 0 where $B(i) = 0$ by using the SNESV instruction. Setting the vector-mask register in this fashion makes the DIVV and SV instructions operate only on elements i of the A and B vectors where $B(i) \neq 0$. Thus, the only elements of $A(i)$ that will be computed and stored are those where the corresponding element $B(i)$ is non-zero.

```
code_1: LV      V1, A(i)        ; load A(i)
        MULTSV  V2, Fx, V1      ; form x*A(i)
        MULTSV  V3, Fy, V1      ; form y*A(i)
        ADDV    V4, V2, V3      ; form x*A(i)+y*A(i)
        SV      A(i), V4        ; save result
```

Figure B.8: Vector Code for FORTRAN Code Sequence 1.

```
code_2: LV      V1, A(i)        ; load A(i)
        MULTSV  V2, Fx, V1      ; form x*A(i)
        SV      A(i), V2        ; save result
```

Figure B.9: Vector Code for FORTRAN Code Sequence 2.

▷ Exercise B.8

The formula for T_n presented on page B–30 of the text has a T_{base} term that was used in the expression for T_n presented in the first edition of the text. T_{base} should not appear in the second edition as the authors have changed the way they compute T_n.

Before solving this exercise, we must first develop DLXV vector code to implement the two FORTRAN code sequences. The DLXV code for the first sequence is shown in Figure B.8, and the DLXV code for the second sequence is shown in Figure B.9.

Both of these sequences do not show the integer code required to handle strip-mining of the loop. In this exercise we will explore the performance of these two sequences on two different versions of DLX. To perform these evaluations, we will need to apply our equation for T_n:

$$T_n = \left\lceil \frac{n}{MVL} \right\rceil (T_{loop} + T_{start}) + nT_{chime} \tag{B.7}$$

This equation represents the time to execute the vector sequence on a vector of length n and is derived in Section B.3 of the text.

▷ Exercise B.8(c)

The first step to complete before we can determine the timing of the second code sequence on DLXV is to partition the vector code presented in Figure B.9 into convoys. With chaining and two load/store units the second code sequence can be partitioned into one convoy on DLXV:

1. All three instructions in the sequence can be chained together. As chaining "eliminates" the data dependence with respect to determining convoy membership and there are no structural hazards (remember, DLXV has two load/store units), the three instructions in the sequence can share a single convoy.

The second code sequence thus executes in one chime on DLXV.

From the FORTRAN source code presented in the exercise statement, the second code sequence processes a total of 100 elements. To find the number of cycles required by this code sequence on DLXV, we compute T_n from Equation B.7 with n equal to 100:

$$T_{100} = \left\lceil \frac{100}{64} \right\rceil (15 + 31) + 100\,(1) = 192$$

where T_{start} is the sum of the start up overhead of the convoy, $12+7+12 = 31$, and T_{loop} is 15 from the exercise statement.

▷ Exercise B.8(d)

The first step to complete before we can determine the timing of the second code sequence on DLXVII is to partition the vector code presented in Figure B.9 into convoys. With chaining, two of each floating-point vector functional unit and two load/store units, the second code sequence can be partitioned into one convoy on DLXVII:

1. All three instructions in the sequence can be chained together. As chaining "eliminates" the data dependence with respect to determining convoy membership and there are no structural hazards (remember, DLXVII has two load/store units), the three instructions in the sequence can share a single convoy.

The second code sequence thus executes in one chime on DLXVII.

From the FORTRAN source code presented in the exercise statement, the second code sequence processes a total of 100 elements. To find the number of cycles required by this code sequence on DLXVII, we compute T_n from Equation B.7 with n equal to 100:

$$T_{100} = \left\lceil \frac{100}{64} \right\rceil [2\,(15 + 31)] + 100\,(1) = 284$$

Where T_{start} is the sum of the start-up overhead of the convoy, $12 + 7 + 12 = 31$, and T_{loop} is 15 from the exercise statement.[7]

In this case, the performance of DLXV is better than that of DLXVII on the second code sequence. This difference can be attributed to the fact that this code does not utilize the additional vector functional units available on DLXVII yet ends up paying the increased overheads required to support this feature. If your workload consisted of codes like the second code sequence, it would not make sense to choose DLXVII over DLXV even though on paper DLXVII looks like it should provide more performance.

▷ Exercise B.10

This exercise explores how source transformations can be applied to make code vectorizable. Although code may appear at first glance to have loop-carried dependences that can prevent vectorization, making slight changes to the source can remove such dependences while preserving the functionality of the original code. Therefore, a smart compiler can expose parallelism that might not be found by a less refined version.[8]

▷ Exercise B.10(a)

There is a loop-carried dependence between the statement `A(i) = B` and the statement `C(i) = A(i-1)`. This dependence arises because the assignment to `C(i)` depends on a value of `A(i)` computed in an earlier iteration.

▷ Exercise B.11

This exercise examines how compiler techniques can be applied to make it possible to vectorize *reductions* using techniques such as *scalar expansion* or *recursive doubling*. This exercise concentrates on the latter technique.

▷ Exercise B.11(a)

To implement the loop from the exercise using recursive doubling, we will set up two nested loops. The idea is to split the vector into two halves,

---

[7]Remember that T_{loop} and T_{start} are doubled on DLXVII due to increased hardware complexity.

[8]Which once again proves that having high-performance hardware *and* software is critical to obtaining the most out of a system.

```
        length = 32
        do 10 i = 1, 6
            do 20 j = 1, length
                dot(j) = dot(j) + dot(j+length)
20          continue
            length = length / 2
10      continue
```

Figure B.10: *FORTRAN Code to Implement a Reduction with Recursive Doubling.*

add them together, and store the result into the first half. Continue to repeat this step but use the first half as the entire vector until the half is a single element. The FORTRAN code that implements the reduction using recursive doubling is shown in Figure B.10.

On the first pass through the **i** loop, we add elements **dot(0)** through **dot(31)** to elements **dot(32)** through **dot(63)** and store the results in elements **dot(0)** through **dot(31)**. On the next iteration, we add elements **dot(0)** through **dot(15)** to elements **dot(16)** through **dot(31)**. We continue in this way until we add **dot(0)** to **dot(1)**. We are left with the reduced value of the **dot()** vector in **dot(1)**.